The

Last Days of
New York

a reporter's true tale

SETH BARRON

Humanix Books
www.humanixbooks.com

Humanix Books

THE LAST DAYS OF NEW YORK
Copyright © 2021 by Seth Barron
All rights reserved.

Humanix Books, P.O. Box 20989, West Palm Beach, FL 33416, USA
www.humanixbooks.com | info@humanixbooks.com

Humanix Books is a division of Humanix Publishing, LLC. Its trademark, consisting of the word "Humanix" is registered in the Patent and
Trademark Office and in other countries.

ISBN: 978-1-63006-187-6 (Hardcover)
ISBN: 978-1-63006-188-3 (E-book)

Printed in the United States of America
10 9 8 7 6 5 4 3 2 1

To the memory of my mother,
and to my father

Contents

Foreword

IT MAY SOMETIMES SEEM that cities, like civilizations, are always on the brink of collapse, threatened by unmanageable complexity, internal strife, and serial misgovernance. Lewis Mumford, in *The Culture of Cities* (1938), foresaw imminent urban disintegration and chaos, an outlook best captured by one of his chapters titled, "A Brief Outline of Hell." Roughly 20 years later, in *The Death and Life of Great American Cities*, Jane Jacobs warned against the strangling effects of the urban planning that was then so fashionable and doing so much harm to small-scale neighborhood life. Only four years ago, Richard Florida, normally a civic booster of Babbitt-like enthusiasm, prophesied doom in *The New Urban Crisis*.

Little wonder, then, that episodes of civic renaissance and vitality are so striking: those fortunate times when things go right. Seth Barron's *The Last Days of New York*—a propulsive chronicle of failed policy and bad leadership—shows that things *did* once go right in New York City, and not so long ago. Under Rudolph Giuliani in the 1990s and Michael Bloomberg in the three mayoral terms that followed, the city found its way again after the dangerous decline of the 1970s and 1980s.

This feat was accomplished by reducing crime, restoring public order, reconquering public spaces, and reanimating neighborhoods. Barron demonstrates just how easily such gains can be lost. He focuses in particular on the unwinding of the quality-of-life policing that made New York newly livable in the late 1990s and early 2000s, luring investors to a city that had faced bankruptcy within living memory. But behind that unwinding were leaders whose rhetoric was poisonous and whose decisions were destructive.

Here pride of place goes to Bill de Blasio, a man whose mayoralty (thankfully now in its last year) is at the center of Barron's narrative. De Blasio's eagerness to appease public-sector unions, support radical protesters, recite woke cliches (not least the ones decrying "racism"), squander vast sums of money on feckless programs, and, most of all, soften or eliminate police procedures essential to fighting crime—all come under Barron's closely detailed scrutiny. And the city itself? More and more, Barron suggests, it is a place of squalor and disorder, with the homeless parked seemingly everywhere and violence on the rise. "After decades of declining crime," he writes, ". . . New York was, seemingly overnight, scary again." Meanwhile, the city's businesses, already under pressure from high taxes and the mayor's "progressive" reforms (paid sick leave, a higher minimum wage), face endless ordeal and possible extinction—a condition that the recent pandemic has only intensified.

What is to be done? Barron, to his credit, offers no soaring visions of a future city that, with just the right mix of policies, will takes its place with Athens and Rome in the annals of municipal glory. But he can't help feeling that New York can do better—indeed, that it *has* done better and has ruinously lost its way. He describes a recent encounter he himself had with a seriously disturbed man in Washington Square Park—a man (it turned out) with a long criminal history who was, at the time, wielding a crossbow and a machete menacingly. The police did come and arrest him, but he was released on his own recognizance right away.

Such incidents, all too familiar to New Yorkers these days, may not amount to "anarchy," a word that Mayor de Blasio vehemently rejects when it is used to describe his city. "But," Barron adds, "it isn't the New York City that Bill de Blasio inherited, either."

Heather Mac Donald

Introduction:
Folly and Collapse

New York City was reeling in the summer of 2020. Riots had broken out after the death of George Floyd in Minneapolis in late May. Violent mobs targeted police officers, and more than 450 cops were injured by anarchists and Black Lives Matter protestors. Hundreds of New York Police Department (NYPD) vehicles were torched, and there were multiple attempts to firebomb occupied police cars. Hundreds of stores were looted of millions of dollars of goods. Unpermitted marches blocking traffic went on almost continuously.

In late June, hundreds of anti-police demonstrators occupied City Hall Park, between City Hall and the Brooklyn Bridge, and pledged not to leave until the city "defunded" the

NYPD in the forthcoming budget. The protestors indicated clearly that they wanted the existing police force disbanded and replaced by community-based conflict-resolution workers. Following passage of the budget, which shifted $1 billion in funding from the NYPD and cut recruitment, the "occupiers" refused to leave. Their camp turned the plaza next to City Hall into a shantytown, with violence, rampant harassment of local residents, and defacement of public and private property.

The month of July saw a shocking rise in violent crime across New York City. The number of shootings, compared with the same period the previous year, increased by 177 percent; the number of murders rose by 59 percent. Burglary, grand larceny, and auto theft were also up significantly. Neighborhoods around the city experienced a spike in street harassment and random assaults; thieves brazenly walked around luxury stores and walked out with whatever they wanted. At the same time, hundreds of thousands of residents were moving out or making plans to, thousands of businesses were closing their doors permanently, and the city was facing a $10 billion budget hole as tax revenue dried up.

In response to this unfolding inexorable disaster, Mayor Bill de Blasio made a bold move. On the morning of July 9, the mayor, joined by his wife, Al Sharpton, and a few dozen supporters, painted "Black Lives Matter" in giant letters on Fifth Avenue, in front of Trump Tower and television cameras. "This is such an important moment for our city," announced de Blasio. "This is something we need to do for New York City, here and all over." The mayor exulted, "We are liberating Fifth Avenue! We are uplifting Fifth Avenue!" Plans were set to paint similar street murals in every borough to celebrate the lost history that "black people built Fifth Avenue, built New York City, built America. They gave people the right to have . . . luxury."

Later that same day, after helping paint the letter "L," de Blasio went on CNN to discuss with Wolf Blitzer the cancellation of all public events for the foreseeable future, because of the pandemic.

> So, no, we don't need big events any time soon. We've had a lot of success making New York City healthier. We've got to really stick to that plan . . . like street fairs. It means, you know, big outdoor concerts, and it means things like parades, you know, things that here in this city can mean not just thousands, tens of thousands, hundreds of thousands of people. It's just not time for that now.

Blitzer then asked de Blasio the very question that many New Yorkers—who had spent the previous four months locked in their apartments, avoiding friends and family, missing graduations and proms, unable to attend the deaths or funerals of their loved ones—were asking: "What about protests? If people want to march down Fifth Avenue, are they going to be allowed to do so?"

The mayor did not miss a beat, segueing directly into the widely expressed contention that some mass gatherings— driven by the demand for racial justice—matter more than others and are therefore exempt from pandemic-related restrictions.

Look, Wolf, this is always an area of real sensitivity. If you're just talking about health, we would always say, hey, folks, you know, stay home if you can. But we understand that this moment in history people are talking about the need for historic changes. I mean, today, in New York City, you know, recognizing the power and the meaning of the message "Black Lives Matter," which we did in front of Trump Tower today—this is a historic moment of change. We have to respect that, but also say to people the kinds of gatherings we're used to, the parades, the fairs, we just can't have that while we're focusing on health right now.

New Yorkers grew accustomed to hearing that despite lockdown and quarantine orders, it was okay to hold marches and rallies, blocking traffic while angrily screaming, because it was demanded by the arc of history. De Blasio repeated this sentiment whenever he was asked about the evident double standard. "We are seeing a national historic moment of pain and anguish, and a deep cry for help and a deep cry for change. It is not your everyday situation," he told a reporter in June, a week after reports emerged that his own daughter Chiara had been arrested at a violent protest on lower Broadway, where police were attacked.

"I love my daughter deeply," he told the world after her mugshot—deranged and wild-eyed, mohawked, with her earlobes gauged out—was published.

I honor her. She is such a good human being. She only wants to do good in the world. She wants to see a better and more peaceful world. She believes a lot of change is needed. I'm proud of her that she cares so much and she was willing to go out there and do something about it.

In her case, "doing something about it" meant joining a mob throwing bottles at cops.

It was hard not to feel that New York City underwent a kind of phase shift in that period: a fundamental transformation in kind that altered the city at the molecular level, more or less permanently. The city was, factually, collapsing. Plainly, the economic pain was going to be deep. The subways had been in major trouble before the pandemic; now, the very continuation of regular service was in serious question. New York City's tourism sector, which hosted 65 million visitors in 2019, cratered; hundreds of thousands of jobs related to hospitality, entertainment, and shopping disappeared.

Morally, New York took on a revolutionary aspect in which agents of chaos and preachers of despair were touted as noble heroes, peace officers—the majority of whom are nonwhite—were derided as racist killers, and average residents were commanded to chant the slogans of the new Red Guard or face reprisal as fascists because "silence equals violence," whereas violence, it seems, equals protected speech. Echoing their colleagues around the country, local politicians and reporters lavishly praised violent mobs as the heirs of Martin Luther King and the acolytes of Gandhi, while they analyzed videos of police engagements with Zapruder-like intensity, hunting for violations of the civil rights of raving anarchists puncturing tires and clubbing cops on the back of the head in the middle of a scrum.

Anyone who could, left. Anyone who couldn't, cowered. To quell nighttime looting, the mayor declared an 8 p.m. curfew; in response, the public advocate—who holds a city-wide position that assumes control in the event the mayor is indisposed—the speaker of the city council, and a clutch of other prominent officials knelt in Times Square at 8:01 p.m. to defy the principle of public order. This crew blustered that de Blasio's belated curfew was ill-advised, probably illegal, and certainly inflammatory. State senator and former city comptroller John Liu said the curfew, which did dampen violence and destruction, "was like throwing gasoline on a fire."

Councilman Mark Levine, chairman of the council's Health Committee, condemned the police, tweeting, "NYPD, your use of tear gas is increasing COVID-19 risk, because it (1) makes the respiratory tract more susceptible to infection, (2) exacerbates existing inflammation, (3) makes people cough. So stop." The NYPD did not use tear gas prior to this tweet, nor after it; Levine did not retract or correct his statement.

New Yorkers were thus forced to endure an absurd, self-serving spectacle, in which Mayor de Blasio accepted the role of the bad guy, supposedly imposing ferocious police state tactics upon placid practitioners of civil disobedience, while the lesser officials, all of whom were seeking reelection or higher office, pretended that they were fighting against fascism. This was not the first iteration of this circus-style dynamic, which both sides regularly exploited for their own purposes. Meanwhile, the city roiled.

When in the future people ask how New York City fell to pieces, they can be told—in the words of

Hemingway—"gradually, then suddenly." New Yorkers awoke from a slumber of ease and prosperity to discover not only that their glorious city was unprepared for crisis but also that the underpinnings of its fortune had been gutted.

Faced with a global pandemic of world-historical proportions, New York's leadership dithered, offering contradictory, unscientific, and meaningless advice. The city and state became the world's epicenter of infection and death. The protests, riots, and looting that followed the death of George Floyd and the resurgence of the Black Lives Matter movement—cheered on and celebrated by the media and political class—accelerated the crash of confidence that New York City needed to rebound quickly from the economic disaster.

Bill de Blasio's failure to manage the outbreak of COVID-19 is well established. But what is less well understood is how poorly he managed the city up to the point of the pandemic and how his mismanagement left New York City vulnerable to the social, economic, and cultural shocks that have leveled its confidence and brought into question its capacity to absorb the creative energies of the world and reflect them back in the form of opportunity and wealth, as it has done for hundreds of years. At a moment when socialist currents are stirring throughout America, Bill de Blasio's term in office in New York City is a demonstration of what those impulses actually produce: debt, decay, and bloat.

1

"Worst Mayor Ever"

PEOPLE LIKE TO SAY that de Blasio is the worst mayor in New York City history. And there's a good case to be made for it. One could argue that Abe Beame (mayor from 1974 to1977) was worse because it was under him that New York essentially went into receivership—but he inherited a dysfunctional city government that was addicted to social spending. David Dinkins (mayor from 1990 to 1993) is definitely in the running because it was under him that murders peaked at over 2,000 annually—but Dinkins took over a city in the throes of the crack wars.

De Blasio, in contrast, inherited a city that was in good working order in 2014. New York City had emerged from the Great Recession much more quickly than other cities.

Tax revenue was pouring in. The streets were safe, with crime low and trending lower. Tourism was booming as New York enjoyed a stellar international reputation. Immigrants continued to flock here from overseas, and so did domestic migrants. The population hit 8 million in 2000 and added another 170,000 over the next decade.

So, in a sense, there wasn't much demanded of de Blasio and the other Progressive Democrats—call their ascendency "the Prog"—who rose to control of New York City in the election of 2013. The ship of state was steady; all they had to do was keep it from taking on water. But de Blasio and the Progressives had campaigned as revolutionaries whose goal was nothing short of the elimination of economic inequality. De Blasio's campaign statement insisted that "400,000 millionaires call New York home, while nearly half of our neighbors live at or near the poverty line. Our middle class isn't just shrinking; it's in danger of vanishing altogether." While it's true that New York is legendarily a tough place to make it, the city's poverty rate is actually lower than that of Boston, Chicago, Los Angeles, Houston, or Philadelphia, not to mention Detroit or Dallas, and its median income runs well ahead of most large cities. The precept that inequality equals misery simply isn't true.

Economic inequality in New York City, which is majority nonwhite, with a large immigrant population, is easily cast in terms of race, and de Blasio's "Two Cities" narrative was readily adaptable to the politics of racial resentment. It is common for advocates to talk about race "as a proxy" for various social ills. Coming to office in the middle of Obama's second term, which was marked by increasing racial consciousness and hostility, de Blasio made every policy in New York—education, housing, health, transit, park access, statues and monuments, environmental sustainability, sanitation infrastructure—about the rectification of racial grievances. Structural economic inequality, which is after all impossible for a municipal official to do much about, gave way to demands for racial "equity," which are amenable to superficial measures and symbolic gestures. Opportunity falls away as a goal in favor of endless harping about unequal outcomes.

Thus, useless, pointless spectacles like painting "Black Lives Matter" on Fifth Avenue, accompanied by highfalutin pontification, are the defining characteristic of the de Blasio years, infecting all levels of New York City government and politics. Easy to do, low cost, forgettable. As his years in office came to their end, New York was less safe, less prosperous, and certainly more divided than it was when he entered City Hall. This makes a powerful argument for his mayoralty as a low point in the history of New York City's executive governance.

It is not the thesis of this book that Bill de Blasio was uniquely responsible for destroying New York. That would be an unfair caricature, and it would also endow de Blasio with a puissance that he frankly does not possess. What this book does detail is how an equity-oriented social ideology yoked to a big-city political machine, fueled by contributions from the real estate industry and public-sector unions recirculating tax revenue, funneled through a corrosive consultant class and supporting an unelected but hugely powerful nonprofit advocacy apparatus, rotted out the foundations of

New York City to the point that it could not sustain itself against collapse when adverse winds began to blow.

Bill de Blasio is a focus of this book because he presided at the tipping point, but like any fulcrum, he has no moment. No one would ascribe forcefulness or gravity to de Blasio: he was a functionary around whom collapse occurred. The "Great Man" theory of history distinctly does not pertain here; this book is about a political culture of which Bill de Blasio was flower, fruit, and fragrance. On the other hand, of course, he's the guy who made the speeches, stood in front of the cameras, and wielded the paint roller that liberated Fifth Avenue. So we can't write a history of the de Blasio years without talking at least a little about the man named Bill de Blasio. What follows is a kind of ideological biography, along with a pen portrait of some aspects of his personality.

. . . .

Warren Wilhelm, Jr., aka Bill de Blasio, was born in 1961 as the third son to Warren and Maria (née de Blasio) Wilhelm, both native New Yorkers; he was raised in Boston. His parents were in their midforties at the time of his birth, somewhat unusual for that era; their advanced ages meant that they had reached adulthood during the Great Depression and were familiar with its widespread economic privation. Bill de Blasio speaks constantly about that era and the stories he was told about it by older relatives, from whom he imbibed the salvific mythology of FDR's New Deal. It is no exaggeration to say that de Blasio talks about the New Deal and the promise of expansive government to answer societal

problems more frequently than he makes any other historical or cultural reference. It's his lodestar.

De Blasio frequently references his mother's family,
who emigrated to the United States from Italy early in the
twentieth century. In his 2015 "State of the City" speech he
stressed the humble roots of his grandmother and her sister,
who started an embroidery company out of their apartment
in 1910. "She did not stumble upon success through luck or
charm; she forged it with hard work and raw grit," he said.

The story is somewhat more complex; by 1915, his grandmother and her sister had turned their house at 205 East
17th Street into a factory where no fewer than 34 people
were working. According to contemporary coverage in
the *New York Times*, his great aunt Imperior was arrested
on charges of "violating regulations relating to smoking
and safety appliances." The arrest came "as a result of an
extensive campaign against fire hazards in the factories
of the city"; Imperior pled guilty to "having an inadequate
fire alarm apparatus." In the period following the Triangle
Shirtwaist Factory fire of 1911, in which 146 garment workers were killed, factory labor conditions and fire prevention had become major issues in New York City. De Blasio
has chosen, understandably, not to emphasize his family's
sweatshop-owning history when he makes speeches about
the exploitation of immigrant workers.

De Blasio's father's family is also interesting, though he
almost never mentions it. His grandfather, Donald Wilhelm,
came from Ohio, graduated from Harvard, and was a published author. He interviewed former President William
Howard Taft for the *New York Times*, knew Theodore

Roosevelt, and was Herbert Hoover's personal secretary. De Blasio's uncle, Donald Wilhelm, Jr., was an intimate of the Shah of Iran and apparently ghostwrote his memoir; the Shah thanks him lavishly in the Preface and calls him a "personal friend as well as a friend of my country."

It seems clear that the Wilhelms had ties to the intelligence establishment and possibly the CIA. Certainly the Shah came to power through a CIA-backed coup shortly before de Blasio's uncle helped him with his book. And de Blasio's father worked for various organizations, such as the Russian Research Center at Harvard, that are known CIA front groups.

De Blasio's parents attended elite colleges, Smith and Yale, at the height of the Depression, which indicates something about their class position, or at least their economic security. They met while working at *Time* magazine in the late thirties. His father lost a leg fighting in the Pacific during World War II and married Maria de Blasio upon his demobilization. After the war, the couple's loyalty came into question when they were seeking federal employment; oddly enough, Maria de Blasio worked under Whittaker Chambers at *Time*, and he apparently reported her as insufficiently patriotic. (Chambers was a former communist and Soviet spy who broke with the party during the great purges of 1938.)

Their local "Loyalty Board" investigated the de Blasios and determined that the couple was not necessarily disloyal but nevertheless sympathetic to Communism. Maria de Blasio's postwar membership in the Progressive Citizens of America, a Communist Party front group denounced by

Eleanor Roosevelt and Arthur Schlesinger, probably didn't help. Warren Wilhelm was denied access to confidential documents, and his career as an intelligence analyst was derailed.

The couple divorced when young Bill de Blasio was eight, and his father, dying of lung cancer, shot himself in a Connecticut motel room ten years later. These traumatic events clearly complicated de Blasio's relationship to his father's memory, as evidenced by his rejection of his birth name. Reportedly always called "Bill" anyway, de Blasio underwent a series of official name changes, first to "Warren de Blasio-Wilhelm" in 1983 and then to "Bill de Blasio" in 2002, interspersed with a number of variations, including "Bill Wilhelm" in a 1983 *Times* article about recent college graduates, and "William Wilhelm" in 1990.

De Blasio has given a number of reasons for changing his name. Speaking to a Harlem church audience in 2016, he credited Malcolm X's *Autobiography* as his inspiration, because he

> felt that my mother's side of the family was the family that brought me up, and I wanted to honor that. I wanted to connect myself to that more deeply. And it was my true self. And—you know—I think there was something about the autobiography that just—it was one of those lightning bolt moments that made me think we all have to find our own definition.

In any case, unshackling himself from his patriarchal slave name, cynics might note, didn't hurt him as he eyed a political future in Brooklyn, where an Italian surname would be a plus, and the Prussian resonances of "Wilhelm" a distinct minus, given the borough's demographics.

Earning a full scholarship, de Blasio went to New York University in Greenwich Village, where he engaged in campus politics and studied political science. After graduation, he won a Truman Scholarship and used it to get a master's degree in Latin American politics at Columbia. In 1987, inspired by the Central American solidarity movement, he took a job at the Maryland-based Quixote Center, a pro-Sandinista social justice organization run by a renegade Jesuit priest.

For leftists in the Reagan era, the fight between the revolutionary communist Nicaraguan government led by Daniel Ortega and the American-backed Contras had a romantic appeal comparable to the Spanish Republican cause in the 1930s and similarly inspired thousands of sympathizers to action. Along with the fight against apartheid, solidarity with the plight of Central American peasants was the major leftist cause of the 1980s.

In 1989, de Blasio went to Nicaragua to distribute supplies blocked by an American embargo against the Sandinista government. His two weeks in the beating heart of world socialism did not disappoint the young radical, who described to the *New York Times* in 2013 an epiphany he had while working in a health clinic in the city of Masaya. A map showing "the precise location of every family in town" was used to track how deeply government indoctrination had spread to each household. "There was something I took away from that," explained de Blasio years later. "How hands-on government has to be, how proactive, how connected to the people it must be," he said.

The principle of home visits to solidify political support and surveil the population is central to communist practice. "Propaganda through individual discussion must be systematically organized as door-to-door agitation and conducted by working groups established for this purpose," reads the *Guidelines on the Organizational Structure of Communist Parties, on the Methods and Content of Their Work*, adopted at the Third Congress of the Communist International, 1921. "Not a single house within the local party organization's area of influence can be left out in this agitation."

Naturally, aspiring totalitarian governments like the Sandinistas dress up surveillance and indoctrination in the guise of providing the people with useful information about health and immunization. But responsible cadre members like Bill de Blasio intuit the broader purpose of "hands-on government": to offer goods and services with one hand and instill discipline and messaging with the other. The same principle is alive today in big-city politics, which attract young idealists to work as "organizers." In fact, the function of the organizer, which puzzles outsiders or people who earn their bread by providing goods or services, is so clearly defined among the Progressive elite that it's often cited as a sufficient qualification for elected office.

It's not tendentious to ascribe powerful collectivist tendencies to de Blasio, who has described himself as a democratic socialist. When he was running for reelection in 2017, for instance, he discussed his feelings about private property.

I think there's a socialistic impulse, which I hear every day, in every kind of community, that they would like things to be planned in accordance to their needs. And I would, too. Unfortunately, what stands in the way of that is hundreds of years of history that have elevated property rights and wealth to the point that that's the reality that calls the tune on a lot of development. . . . Look, if I had my druthers, the city government would determine every single plot of land, how development would proceed.

Maybe de Blasio was just being provocative or especially candid when he said this, but it's basically the most radical statement about the state, progress, and property that one could hear from a major elected American politician. There's nothing vaguely "democratic" about this kind of socialism; in fact, it would be a challenge to discern a dime's worth of difference between de Blasio's land-use "druthers" as expressed here and the expropriative policies of any hard-core communist regime throughout the twentieth century.

· · · · · · · · · ·

Returning to America, de Blasio began his political career in earnest in 1989, helping organize the vote for David Dinkins's successful mayoral run. Later, de Blasio worked in City Hall as an aide to deputy mayor Bill Lynch. It was while working in that job that de Blasio met his future wife, Chirlane McCray, who worked as a Dinkins speechwriter. McCray, seven years de Blasio's senior, was an open lesbian who had published a major article in *Essence* magazine titled, "I Am a Lesbian."

Undeterred, or perhaps provoked, by the challenge, de Blasio pursued his lady love tirelessly, despite her protestations of disinterest. The *Times* reported

> He flirted with her mercilessly . . . calling nonstop and trying to steal an unwelcome kiss. "I actually told him, 'Slow this down,'" Ms. McCray said. Her resistance became less diplomatic: "Back off."

In today's workplace, it would seem less than charming for a man to pester a lesbian colleague to date him, but in the City Hall of the early 1990s the mores were different, apparently.

Chirlane McCray was an original signatory to the 1977 "Combahee River Collective Statement." The Combahee River Collective was a Boston-area black lesbian socialist consciousness-raising group that propounded an early version of contemporary "intersectional" thinking about race, gender, and class. The statement is cited by the black lesbian founders of Black Lives Matter as a crucial source and influence.

The couple married in 1994. Sal Albanese, a Brooklyn councilman from 1983 until 1998—who twice challenged de Blasio for the Democratic nomination for mayor—recalls attending the wedding.

> He invited me to his wedding in Prospect Park. We got along I guess; I encountered him when he was Bill Lynch's assistant. He would deal with councilmember requests. He

would be out there with a pencil and notebook, and nothing would happen . . . he was totally ineffective. The pattern hasn't changed!

Anyway, it was an outdoor wedding, very hot day. We are all sitting there sweating. He showed up an hour and a half late to his own wedding. I remember sitting with my wife, his two aunts who were Italian sitting behind me, talking. Now I'm from Italy, so I could understand what they were saying. One of the aunts says, in Italian, "Bill was an asshole when he was a kid and he's still an asshole."

Plus ça change . . . de Blasio acquired a reputation for tardiness early in his mayoralty and never shook the impression that he tends to slack off.

Following their honeymoon in Castro's Cuba—in violation of a ban on travel—de Blasio and McCray had two children, Chiara and Dante. It would impute fiendish cynicism to suggest that marrying a black woman and having biracial children was part of de Blasio's long plan to run for office, but it is certainly true that he has used his family to political advantage, centering them in his many campaigns since he was elected to the local school board in 1999. His victory in the 2013 Democratic primary was widely credited, only semihumorously, to his teenaged son's Afro, which became a media sensation.

De Blasio and McCray were aggressive about using their children as props, highlighting Chiara's depression and substance abuse in pushing McCray's mental-wellness initiatives and Dante's experiences as a young black man dealing with the police. Neither example, in fact, was especially instructive. Publicizing Chiara's recovery from drug addiction appears not to have prevented her from relapsing, and Dante's *New York Times* op-ed about a confrontation with the police in San Francisco described how a police car slowed down as he was opening the door of a house he was visiting—hardly a case study in brutality.

De Blasio's parading of his family irked black politicians, who found it condescending. Charles Barron, a former Black Panther who was in the city council with de Blasio and who is known for his unapologetic race-conscious politics, called him out in 2009 during his run for public advocate, when the de Blasio campaign was accused of targeting black neighborhoods with flyers depicting his wife and kids, while white neighborhoods got pamphlets with pictures of de Blasio alone. "The insulting part of it is that if you want to appeal to the black community, then appeal to us based upon our issues, not based upon who you're married to," said Barron at the time. More recently, Jumaane Williams, the current public advocate, slammed de Blasio for what he called overaggressive policing in the wake of the George Floyd riots. "This is me talking, like, you can no longer hide behind your black wife and children, not anymore," said Williams.

Pandering aside, it's obvious that the de Blasios, man and wife, were made for politics, because it is unclear that they could have made a living doing anything else. Before getting elected, de Blasio was a political operative with good connections, including his first cousin John Wilhelm, a major union boss, and Harold M. Ickes, the son of FDR's interior secretary. After his underwhelming work in the Dinkins administration, de Blasio managed Charles Rangel's 1994 reelection, more or less a walkover: it's instructive to note that neither Dinkins nor Rangel endorsed de Blasio for mayor in 2013. De Blasio then managed Bill Clinton's New York State 1996 reelection campaign, another walkover, and then worked briefly for the city council. He got a job in the second Clinton administration as an assistant to Andrew Cuomo, the secretary of housing and urban development. In none of these jobs did he distinguish himself. In 1999, de Blasio was hired to manage Hillary Clinton's campaign for Senate; reportedly, his performance was subpar and he had to be moved to the side. In 2001, while making money as a "consultant" for the massive SEIU 1199 healthcare workers union, he ran for city council and won. After a decade of steady hustling as a political hack, he was getting a salary straight from the taxpayer and couldn't be fired. Finally, he was able to relax.

While de Blasio was never a productive employee, he could be charming. Testy, irritable, and quick to blame his subordinates, he can be witty, ingratiating, and amiable to people above him or to people he wants something from. One staffer who worked closely with de Blasio in his 2009 run for public advocate relates that he and the candidate were walking around the Marcy Projects in Brooklyn, introducing de Blasio to potential voters. A resident came up to de Blasio and said, "Hey! I know you—you're the guy who likes black pussy!" Without pause, de Blasio retorted, "Sir, I like all pussy."

Whatever one thinks about the man, this aperçu is in the first rank of political quips and comebacks, up there practically with Churchill, Kennedy, or Emperor Charles V. De

Blasio excels at chummy give-and-take and in this sense is a natural politician. He's no dummy; he's just kind of a jerk.

. . . .

One defining characteristic of the de Blasio years has been his shamelessness about pandering to various constituencies. Sometimes his pandering had an absurdist, even "meta" quality, because it didn't even seem like it was to anyone's benefit. For instance, in April 2017, de Blasio staged a ceremony outside City Hall in order to redeem a stain on the history of the city: the fact that Dwight "Doc" Gooden missed the 1986 tickertape parade celebrating the Mets' World Series victory. To "right that wrong," the mayor announced plans to "celebrate [Gooden], who was unable to attend" the original parade, and to "honor" him, with the Key to the City no less.

Why was Gooden unable to attend the original celebration, necessitating a reenactment 31 years later? Was he on a humanitarian mission or tending to a dying relative? As the famed pitcher explained to ESPN in 2011, he was holed up in a drug den, gripped by paranoid hallucinations from doing too much cocaine.

[A] lot of times I get to a certain point of using drugs, the paranoia sticks in. So I end up leaving the party with the team, going to these projects, of all places in Long Island. Hang out there. Then you know what time you have to be at the ballpark to go into the city for the parade, but I'm thinking, "OK, I got time." And the clocks, I mean the rooms are spinning. I said, "OK, I'll leave in another hour." Then the next thing you know the parade's on and I'm watching the parade on TV. Here I am in the projects in a drug dealer's apartment with guys I don't even know, with drugs in the house, watching it. It's a horrible feeling.

The mayor calls Gooden's tale "a story of redemption" and complains that "there wasn't necessarily the opportunity back in 1986 for [him] to enjoy everything [he] had achieved"—including an opportunity to attend the parade—because "other issues were roiling about." By de Blasio's logic, Gooden had nothing to do with his own cocaine binge: it somehow intervened and made him "unable" to show up for the parade. In fact, the mayor touts Gooden's story as a demonstration of "the power of redemption."

But Doc Gooden is hardly a poster child for recovery from drug addiction. During his baseball career—notable for phenomenal early success followed by rapid decline—Gooden was suspended repeatedly for cocaine use. He has relapsed serially since then, getting arrested and convicted many times for driving drunk, punching his girlfriend, and endangering a child, most recently in 2010. In 2006, Gooden volunteered to serve time in prison instead of going on probation because he didn't trust himself not to relapse. In 2019, two years after de Blasio gave him the Key to the City and called him a redemptive model, Gooden was arrested twice, for possession of drug paraphernalia and for driving under the influence.

If Gooden had gone straight after missing the original parade, and perhaps spent some time helping people overcome their addictions, one might make sense of the weird reenactment, which even included celebratory bunting and signage hung outside City Hall. But even if Mayor de Blasio felt that it was somehow sad and undeserved that Gooden had missed the 1986 parade, someone should have reminded him that he did go on to win two more World Series rings, in 1996 and 2000, when he pitched for the Yankees and was able to participate in championship parades for those victories.

Reenacting a parade for Dwight Gooden for no reason was a minor event, but it spoke to a perverse side of Bill de Blasio's character, which is an almost insouciant disregard for the opinions of other people. For most of his mayoralty, de Blasio made it a practice, virtually every morning, to go to his old neighborhood in Brooklyn to ride a stationary bike at the local YMCA, after which he liked to get a pastry and coffee at a favorite café. This ritual required a caravan of SUVs to accompany the mayor and his round-the-clock NYPD security detail. Asked about the efficiency of this daily trip from an environmental standpoint, when his Gracie Mansion residence is a five minute walk from Asphalt Green, a renowned fitness center owned and operated by the city, de Blasio dismissed these objections as "emotional appeals" and "bait."

He explained that the "issue is not cheap symbolism here" and also said that he never rides the subway because "in the end people want to make sure that I'm getting things done for them all the time and so that's the first imperative here . . . the number one thing I owe the people is good use of my time." Going to the Y to pedal desultorily on an exercycle every midmorning, while most people are at work, was in de Blasio's mind a "good use" of his time, one that the people of New York would appreciate, if they were sensible.

Chirlane McCray, telling *New York* magazine about her daily schedule, including the daily trip to the gym in Park Slope, explained, "Well, you know, it seems like it's quite a hike from the Upper East Side, but the ride to Park Slope is really just 20, 25 minutes," which is especially true when your SUV is waiting for you, is driven by an NYPD detective after rush hour ends, and drops you off at the door to the gym. McCray described how "[w]e really love our Y—we've been going there for decades. I also go to the dry cleaners and pharmacy there, which is very grounding." Being chauffeured 20 miles roundtrip to a favorite dry cleaner isn't most people's idea of "grounding," but elections have consequences, after all.

In the same interview, McCray revealed that she and Mayor de Blasio were in the process of watching a favorite TV series—again. "Right now, we're rewatching *The Wire*—we're in the third season. I never thought I'd watch the whole thing all over again but it's totally worth doing." New Yorkers were relieved to learn that the legendarily second-hardest job in America includes ample time for reruns.

One of the most absurd episodes in de Blasio's career occurred in 2015, when both parties were gearing up for a contentious primary season for the upcoming national election. De Blasio decided to play kingmaker by withholding his endorsement of Hillary Clinton, even though he had worked for her and her husband, who joined him on stage at his 2013 inauguration at City Hall and swore him in. For six months, through the spring and summer of 2015, de Blasio refused to endorse Clinton, claiming that he was waiting to "learn more about" the policy vision of a woman whose senatorial campaign he had run. Later, pushing to establish himself as the voice of the party's left, he tried to sponsor a summit on economic inequality, inviting candidates from both parties; none of them agreed to attend.

In January 2016, de Blasio and his wife went to Iowa to campaign for Clinton, though she and her staff froze him out. Images of the trip show the mayor and McCray walking by themselves down deserted suburban streets holding clipboards. Then, at the Democratic National Convention in July, he was given possibly the worst speaking slot—the afternoon of the third day, right before the "In Memoriam" slideshow of recently deceased Democrats. The symbolism was hard to miss.

When the city's subways were melting down in 2017, causing delays and miserable commutes for tens of thousands of straphangers, de Blasio assumed and embraced the role of a hapless bystander, shrugging his shoulders at what he insisted was not his problem. "If you have a concern—if you like something NYPD is doing, or you don't like it—talk to me. If you like the schools or you don't like them, talk to me," explained de Blasio on his weekly radio appearance. "If you like something happening in our subways or don't like it, you talk to the governor."

The mayor continued on this theme for more than a year, reveling in his lack of responsibility for the backbone of the city's economy. "The city of New York—number one responsibilities include policing, fire department, schools;

all the things that affect daily of life of the people—public hospitals, etc.," he explained, relishing his freedom from care. "The MTA—unless the governor wants to turn the MTA over to the city of New York—the MTA is the state's responsibility."

While it's technically true that the mayor does not control the MTA, there are certainly things he could do to improve it, but more important, it was bizarre to see the city's chief executive constantly and gleefully disavow any obligation for such a core element of New York's infrastructure. No mayor in city history ever made such a virtue of his incapacity.

At the time, de Blasio's campaign for the presidency in the 2020 election, which he announced in May 2019, seemed like utter folly. Nobody thought it was a good idea; it was like a terrible joke. But in retrospect, after the calamity that befell New York when COVID-19 hit, his fatuous run for the highest office seems grotesque—an obscene waste of time.

A few days before the official kickoff of his candidacy, de Blasio staged a press conference at Trump Tower to announce the "New York City Green New Deal." The mayor said he was putting Donald Trump on notice "because his buildings are among the biggest polluters in New York City." According to de Blasio, buildings are major contributors to climate change because of their carbon emissions. "You know what's crazy?" he asked. "Buildings destroying the future for our children and grandchildren."

Because it was raining that day, de Blasio chose to hold his press conference-cum-kickoff rally in the lobby of Trump Tower—the very belly of the beast—which is open to the public. The event, which was supposed to be a shot across the bow warning then-President Trump that de Blasio had him in his sights, turned into a circus. With the mayor positioned in front of the infamous Trump Tower escalator, cameras captured anti–de Blasio protestors riding it up and down with signs reading "WORST MAYOR EVER" and "DE BLASIO RESIGN," blowing whistles, and forcing him to yell to be heard.

De Blasio's war on buildings was about as silly as it sounds. The problem with trying to greenify New York is that the city has little heavy industry polluting the atmosphere, mass transit is already the primary mode of transportation, and people live compactly with a low carbon footprint. So de Blasio and the Progressives in city government targeted buildings, which are the city's largest producer of greenhouse gas emissions. But it's not the buildings that produce greenhouse gases so much as it is the activity that goes on inside buildings—energy to run heating and cooling systems, power computers, and provide light for workers and residents.

In any event, de Blasio's run for higher office was an exercise in egoism. Reporters who covered his travels noted how much lighter and effusive he seemed on the trail, dressing in hipper clothes, hiking around Red Rock Canyon in Nevada, glad-handing people who were unfamiliar with his laugh lines and general shtick. It was good to get away from his day job, with crime on the rise, the subways falling apart, and homeless mentally ill people taking over the streets of Manhattan. One could see what a downer it was for him to have to come back to work after his adventure on the national stage came to an end. But if he expected to return and just ride out the last 15 months of his time in office, he was in for a jolt.

2

Policing New York: The Progressive War on Safety

ONE LATE SUMMER SUNDAY morning, Demetrius Harvard, a 30-year-old Bronx man, stood on a subway platform in Greenwich Village and methodically threw construction material onto the tracks. Bystanders tried to stop him, and someone even went into the train well to remove the debris, but Harvard persisted in his sabotage. Eventually, he succeeded in derailing an uptown A train, injuring several passengers.

You had to read to the end of tabloid news reports to get the real story. Two weeks earlier, in the same neighborhood, Harvard had tossed a steel bench through a bus window. He was arrested, charged with criminal mischief, and immediately "ROR'd"—released on his recognizance—with no bail.

This cycle is now all too common in New York, where public order and safety have been buffeted by chaotic forces. Criminal justice reform at the state level removed bail as an option for all but the most heinous charges. Locally, the NYPD has stopped enforcing many quality-of-life laws. The city council passed a law forbidding cops from applying pressure to the chest or back of an arrestee while trying to handcuff him or her, on the premise that this tactic is tantamount to asphyxiation; officers dealing with a resisting suspect would thus potentially face assault charges if they attempt to restrain him or her with vigor.

The COVID-19 pandemic led to the release of inmates from jails and prisons across New York. "The number of New Yorkers held in NYC jails has plummeted, shrinking by 27% in ten weeks, a steeper population decline than in all of last year," boasted the mayor's Office of Criminal Justice. "The jail population is at a number not seen since 1946."

That would be great news if the incarcerated population were tracking the crime rate, but the exact opposite was true. Crime is up dramatically, as released inmates, now adjusted to a climate of permissiveness, resume criminal activity. Advocates for reform sneered at the suggestion that bail reform or pandemic-related releases were responsible for the lawless surge, but arrests have plummeted across the city. It goes against common sense to assume that the rise in crime has nothing to do with the release of thousands of career criminals into the community.

After decades of declining crime and a general feeling of carefree personal security among an entire generation of New Yorkers unfamiliar with triple-locked doors, widespread graffiti, carrying "mugger money," and avoiding parks after dark, New York was, seemingly overnight, scary again. Murders in 2020 jumped some 39 percent over the previous year, and shootings more than doubled, as gangs felt free to blast away at each other in the open over obscure beefs and shows of disrespect. The COVID-19 lockdown capped the number of muggings, simply because fewer people were outside, but crime on the subway surged, even while ridership dropped to a tiny fraction of where it had been in normal times.

Weekends in New York began to tally Chicago-style victim numbers: 15 shot one weekend; 25 another. A baby was among four people shot at a cookout in Brooklyn one Sunday night; he died from his wounds. When the police finally identified his killers, it turned out they were already in jail, having been apprehended for murdering someone else.

Meantime, as New York City lapsed into chaos, its feckless leadership did little but sigh. Mayor de Blasio blamed "dislocation in communities," stemming from the coronavirus, but as for what's causing the disorder, he said that he is "much more interested in the solutions rather than continually debating the analysis." Following the 2020 Labor Day weekend, he spoke with pride of how "only" six people were shot in Central Brooklyn, the traditional location of the West Indian Day Parade, which was not held because of the pandemic; one of the wounded was a little boy whose femur was shattered.

But how did this happen, and why? A secure and prosperous city does not go to hell overnight, any more than the collapse of Rome occurred suddenly. As a point of reference, Newark, New Jersey, just a few miles west of New

York and long Gotham's dysfunctional step-sibling, saw a 0 percent increase in its murder rate between 2019 and 2020. Newark also had a terrible experience with the pandemic and certainly has equally deep-rooted social problems. But New York City had the bad ideas of Bill de Blasio, which accompanied by terrible execution set into play forces of undoing that disintegrated the joists and supports of New York's safety, prosperity, and future.

On a sweltering July day in 2014, six months into de Blasio's mayoralty, police detectives on Staten Island approached local resident Eric Garner, on Bay Street, a major commercial thoroughfare near the ferry terminal. Standing several inches over six feet tall and approaching 400 pounds, the 42-year-old Garner was a familiar presence in the area, where he made his living selling loose, untaxed cigarettes—a common and profitable street "hustle."

Having already been arrested dozens of times, on a variety of charges, Garner was well known to the police—and he knew them well, too. Local storekeepers had lodged numerous complaints with the local precinct about illegal sales of drugs and "loosies," and cops routinely patrolled the area to enforce the low-level yet persistent violations of the law that were classified as quality-of-life (QoL) crimes.

When Garner saw the police that day, he reacted adversely, brushing them off. "Every time you see me, you want to mess with me," he told the plainclothes officers who advised him he was being arrested for selling loose cigarettes. "I'm tired of it. It stops today. . . . I'm minding my business, officer, I'm minding my business. Please just leave me alone. I told you the last time, please just leave me alone." Video captured at the scene shows that as the police moved to handcuff the obese, asthmatic, and diabetic Garner, he resisted their efforts, swatting their hands away. "Please, please, don't touch me. Do not touch me," he insisted.

Officer Daniel Pantaleo, observing that Garner was not going to consent to be handcuffed, grabbed the much larger man around the neck, presumably to gain leverage, and pulled him to the ground. Garner struggled with Pantaleo and several other officers, who wrestled with him to get his hands cuffed behind his back. "I can't breathe," said Garner at least 11 times. He fell silent, was placed in an ambulance, and died on his way to the hospital, seemingly of a heart attack brought on by chronic asthma. His massively enlarged heart and apparent pulmonary edema, evidenced by his "visibly swollen ankles," as the New York Times reported, contributed to his death, according to the medical examiner.

The death of Eric Garner became a major, iconic moment in the national rise of the Black Lives Matter movement, which adopted Eric Garner's last words—"I can't breathe"— as a motto and a general statement of black asphyxiation in the airless lunar environment of white supremacy. In New York, Garner's death emerged as a flash point, especially after a grand jury refused to indict Pantaleo later that year and the US Justice Department declined to pursue charges in the matter in 2019. It became standard among the city's leadership to speak of Garner as having been "choked to death," as Al Sharpton put it, or "murdered," in the words of numerous city elected officials.

In the years since Garner died after ordering the police to leave him alone while they tried to conduct a legal arrest, authorized by their commanders, radicals have transformed his truculence into a heroic moment of resistance to injustice, and he has been celebrated as a martyr. "It stops today," pronounced Garner grandiosely, and this declaration was labeled "prophetic" by local councilwoman Debi Rose. "It stops today" has become a kind of rallying cry among anti-police activists and a statement of righteousness—like Martin Luther proclaiming, "Here I stand," or Martin Luther King saying, "Free at last."

But in what moral universe does a career petty criminal get to tell the police to go away?

A few weeks after Garner's death, in similar circumstances, Mike Brown was killed by police officer Darren Wilson in Ferguson, Missouri. Wilson confronted Brown after a shopkeeper reported a strong-arm robbery of a box of cigars; Brown apparently tried to steal Wilson's weapon and then charged the officer. He was shot dead.

Eric Garner's and Mike Brown's deaths became heavily mythologized, well beyond the squalid and less-than-heroic facts of their cases. Mike Brown's friend claimed that he raised his hands in front of Officer Wilson and shouted, "Hands up, don't shoot!"—a claim that was disputed by every other eyewitness and inconsistent with forensic evidence, which demonstrated that Brown had certainly grabbed for Wilson's gun and had been charging him when he was shot. Nonetheless, "Hands up, don't shoot" and "I can't breathe" have become key slogans of the Black Lives Matter movement, which contends that the American system of public safety is a rigged game aimed at controlling—and murdering—black people.

Eric Garner's death, like Mike Brown's, serves as a litmus test about attitudes toward policing and registers the sharp national divide that continues to polarize America. The stark difference in opinion about who's at fault and the very facts of the case—even though the whole episode was captured on video and should be easy to understand—demonstrate the extent to which passion overwhelms reason when it comes to questions of public safety.

The Garner case is central to understanding how 25 years of declining crime and improving public safety in New York City reversed—seemingly overnight—in 2020, following the COVID-19 lockdown and the ensuing George Floyd protests. Eric Garner's death represented the convergence of key themes that have haunted policing in New York City for decades: enforcement of QoL or "minor" crimes, use of force, alleged police racism, how cops are punished, and how communities are policed to begin with.

· · · · · · · · · ·

Bill de Blasio foregrounded police reform in his run for mayor in 2013. He touted himself as uniquely positioned—in large part because of his status as the "father of a black son"—to tackle the supposedly racist policies of the NYPD. It is telling that de Blasio was endorsed by George Soros, whose financial support of anti-cop defense bar radicals in taking over prosecutorial offices around the country—from St. Louis to San Francisco to Philadelphia—has undermined public safety to disastrous effect. In a real sense, Soros's support of de Blasio was a prelude to the carpet of chaos the mogul and his foundations, stuffed with billions of dollars, have rolled out in the ensuing years.

To understand where New York was at the moment of Eric Garner's death, we need to look back to where the city had been decades before, when Gotham, like many large cities, was trapped in a vicious and climbing spiral of violent crime. Starting in the 1960s, urban decay began to fester throughout New York. The causes are many and fiercely argued over. Suffice to say that a decline in manufacturing and shipping-related jobs, which had always provided solid middle-class wages for people without much formal education, in combination with the exodus of white ethnics to the suburbs, began to hollow out the city's tax base.

At the same time, the city's liberal leadership expanded the provision of welfare benefits, thereby creating a dependent underclass mostly comprised of African Americans and Puerto Ricans, who arrived in northern cities in large numbers mostly after World War II. Though part of Harlem was known as a black neighborhood as early as the 1920s, the black population of New York City as a whole remained relatively small for many years. New York was 90 percent white as late as 1950, and non-Hispanic whites comprised an absolute majority of the city until the early 1980s.

By the middle-to-late 1960s, areas of New York City, including the South Bronx, the Lower East Side, and parts of Brooklyn, had taken on extreme slum characteristics. So-called white flight led to a cratering of real estate values. Landlords began to abandoned apartment buildings they could no longer keep up because the rent rolls would not cover maintenance and taxes. Arson—whether by owners for insurance purposes, by tenants for relocation allowances from the city, or by firebugs for kicks—created wastelands of rubble that could stretch for blocks. Images of the Bronx from that time resemble bombed-out postwar Berlin.

Violent crime began to creep up throughout the 1960s, for a variety of reasons. Connecting crime to social or "root" causes is always a tricky business. During the Great Depression, for instance, when hundreds of people were living in shantytown encampments in the middle of Central Park and thousands more of the dispossessed were living in makeshift huts in alleys throughout the city, crime was relatively low. In 1940, for instance, there were only 275 murders, in a population of 7.5 million persons. By the mid-1960s, there were more than twice as many murders each year, even though the population had edged up only to 7.8 million people.

In 1969, there were more than 1,000 murders in New York City, and the number began to climb steadily over the next 20 years. New York became a frightening city, and not only because murder was on the rise. All the major "index crimes" saw sharp increases: rape more than doubled, robbery went up by a factor of five, and aggravated assault more than tripled. And those figures represent only crimes that were reported.

But in addition to the major crimes they reported to the police, New Yorkers were beset by a deterioration in the fabric of life that undercut everything that allows a community to flourish and life to be pleasant. Graffiti covered subway trains, monuments, and ordinary buildings; "bombers" would compete to deface each other's work. Stolen cars were stripped and left to rust in marginal areas or set on fire. City parks were dangerous and unpleasant. Prostitution flourished openly, as did drug dealing, gambling, and public intoxication. Outside of elite neighborhoods, the city was dirty, and life could be harsh.

It was in this period—the 1970s—that Bill de Blasio's future wife Chirlane McCray moved to New York. She speaks wistfully about that period. "I came to New York City in 1977," she reminisced in 2015, "and the city was strong, the city was inclusive and dynamic, and we want the city to stay that way." She and her husband, we will see, have made significant strides toward returning the city to that "inclusive and dynamic" Golden Age.

Starting in the period after World War II, policing—which in large American cities had been dominated by particular ethnic groups and served a patronage function within ruling political machines—became more professionalized. The new ethic of policing was better training, hiring according to a civil service model, and centralized administration. The days of the beat cop patrolling neighborhoods on foot gave way to the radio car, with officers responsible for much broader areas that they knew less intimately. This system, which isolated police in their cars for much of the time, led to rising tensions between police and the communities they were assigned to protect.

Police became tasked largely with waiting for crime to happen and then racing to the scene of the crime after someone called 911. The idea of crime prevention became thought of as the purview of social workers, while real police work meant responding rapidly to serious crime and catching bad guys in the act. Dealing with community concerns, general disorder, or low-level misdemeanors was considered unserious and even a waste of time. The police should be out catching murderers, rapists, and drug kingpins, not breaking up dice games or collaring shoplifters.

But by the early 1980s it was clear that chasing after serious crime wasn't doing much to stop it. The crack epidemic led to an intensification of violence that saw 2,245 murders in 1990, or more than 6 per day. The number that year was inflated, but only marginally, by the 87 people who were murdered in a blaze at the Happy Land Social Club that was set by a jealous boyfriend of a coat checker at the Bronx dance hall, which was operating illegally. That same year, dozens of livery cab drivers—who largely operated in the crime-ridden outer boroughs—were murdered, never for more than $100, often for far less. A quarter of all drivers walked away from their jobs rather than risk getting killed.

High-profile violent confrontations fixed the national image of New York as a place of brutal, random disorder. A Diana Ross concert in July 1983, held in Central Park, turned into a melee, with gangs of "youths" attacking, robbing, and beating other attendees after the show ended. A mob invaded Tavern on the Green, just off Sheep Meadow, knocking over tables and assaulting diners. Dozens were injured and dozens arrested.

A few days before Christmas 1984, a white computer engineer named Bernhard Goetz, who had been mugged three years before, got on the downtown 2 train and took a seat. Four black teenagers surrounded him and demanded five dollars; Goetz swiftly pulled out an unlicensed revolver and fired, wounding all of them, one of them grievously. His 1987 criminal trial resulted in not guilty verdicts on the most serious charges; Goetz was convicted only on a weapons charge. Many New Yorkers hailed Goetz as a hero, though others insisted he was a vigilante targeting blacks to realize depraved fantasies of power.

The Central Park jogger case of April 1989 shocked the world with the nightmarish scene of dozens of teenagers rampaging through the park in the late evening, beating up cyclists and pedestrians, with at least some of them raping and maiming a jogger and leaving her for dead. On a September evening the following year, a family of tourists from Utah got on the subway in Manhattan, planning to take a short trip uptown to have dinner. They were attacked by a gang of teenagers, who mugged and beat the parents, and then stabbed their 22-year-old son, Brian Watkins, to death. These two crimes horrified the nation and set the tone—fairly or not—for the single term of New York City's first black mayor, David Dinkins.

Amid this desperate spiral of violence, a new, counterintuitive vision of crime prevention was born. In 1982, George Kelling and James Q. Wilson published a seminal essay in *The Atlantic* magazine entitled, "Broken Windows: The Police and Neighborhood Safety." The authors argued that the radio-car strategy of policing was a failure because it was reactive. "Patrol cars arrive," they explained, "an occasional arrest occurs but crime continues and disorder is not abated."

In a later article, Kelling made the simple but revolutionary observation that "fear of crime is one of the worst consequences of crime." When ordinary citizens live in fear of crime—which even in the worst of times strikes only a small minority of the population—their lives are crippled. "For every person mugged in the park there are hundreds or thousands who do not walk in the park," Kelling noted. "For every one mugged or robbed in the neighborhood, there are hundreds who triple-bolt their doors and abandon the streets, many others who sell out or do not move in."

Kelling went further, asserting that disorder, or evidence that a neighborhood is out of control ("youths hanging out on the corner; panhandlers, hustlers, and suggestively dressed prostitutes on the street; public drunkenness and rowdiness"), is just as important as "real" crime in instilling fear into ordinary law-abiding people who just want to live their lives securely. Low-level lawlessness like graffiti or drug use signals the absence of authority.

Kelling and Wilson famously put forth what came to be known as the "broken windows" theory of crime. According to them, disorder leads to crime. They wrote

> If a window in a building is broken and is left unrepaired, all the rest of the windows will soon be broken. . . . [O]ne unrepaired broken window is a signal that no one cares, and so breaking more windows costs nothing. (It has always been fun.)

Broken windows theory owes a debt to sociologist, and later US senator, Daniel Patrick Moynihan, who spoke of the way in which cities "define deviancy down." That is, the bar of acceptability is ratcheted down as disorder spreads so that last year's scandal slowly becomes this year's norm.

From this perspective, the way to fight crime isn't so much to chase after serious criminals after they've struck so much as it is to promote orderliness at the neighborhood level—to make it clear that disorder and antisocial behavior are not tolerated. Establishing public order doesn't start with preventing rape and murder; it begins way down the criminological food chain at vandalism.

Kelling and Wilson called for cities to get cops out of their patrol cars.

> In a car, an officer is more likely to deal with street people by rolling down the window and looking at them. The door and the window exclude the approaching citizen; they are a barrier.

Cops walking the street, in the prewar "night watchman" model of policing, were able to interact more directly with neighborhood residents, absorb the local flavor, and become integrated with the flow of information.

Broken windows theory is commonly misunderstood as demanding all-or-nothing Gestapo-style policing and hard punishment for rulebreakers. But the core principle of broken windows theory is that orderly neighborhoods are self-sustaining and that the condition of order fosters a virtuous cycle. As Kelling wrote, "If you want to prevent crime, waiting for it to happen and then stopping it may not work. If you restore order, people will be less fearful, use the streets and maintain [order] themselves." This speaks, too, to the fundamental idea of celebrated urbanist Jane Jacobs, who idealized the "eyes on the street" of functional mixed-use neighborhoods that promote heavy pedestrian traffic. People keeping an eye out, both on and for each other, creates safe streets without the need for a crushing police presence.

An early effort at getting control of the city's disorder was aimed at "squeegee men," who would gather outside tunnel entrances or at red lights and begin, unbidden, to wash motorists' windshields, sometimes with a squeegee, sometimes with a rag and spritz bottle. This dubious service was followed by a demand for a "tip," which wasn't really considered optional—many car antennas and windshield wipers were torn off when drivers refused to hand over some change or folding money. New Yorkers of a certain age remember flicking on their wipers to signal "No" when raggedy men—the type who, homeless or not, used to be called "bums"—lurched toward their cars.

The squeegee men were obnoxious and, unlike most panhandlers, often explicitly threatening—there were many stories of attacks against drivers or fights between squeegee men arguing over turf. Moreover, while laws against vagrancy—statutes that criminalized status rather than specific behaviors—had been largely declared unconstitutionally vague by the Supreme Court in the early 1970s, there was no question that harassing drivers and demanding money for a bogus service were illegal. The squeegee men were universally unpopular and open to attack.

Ed Koch began cracking down on the squeegee men in the 1980s, and his successor, David Dinkins, continued to suppress the practice. In the last year of his administration, Dinkins appointed Ray Kelly as police commissioner. Kelly, a believer in community policing, added thousands of new cops to the streets and further cracked down on the squeegee men. Murder and crime were major issues in the 1993 election, which former prosecutor Rudy Giuliani, running on a law-and-order platform, won in a close race.

Mayor Giuliani, along with his police commissioner William Bratton—who served as the head of the city's transit police starting in 1990—initiated a true revolution in public safety, one that history has not yet had the distance to appreciate properly. Rather than focusing on major crimes, which are hard to predict and prevent, the NYPD made a strategic choice to prevent lower-level disorder. "We start with the premise of the broken windows theory—it is important to maintain a sense of order, and for people to feel the public spaces are available to them," explained Jeremy Travis, deputy commissioner of police for legal matters in the Dinkins years. "Our belief is that if you take care of the little things, the big things will follow."

In their 1994 white paper, "Police Strategy No. 5: Reclaiming the Public Spaces of New York," Giuliani and Bratton set forth their plan to drive low-level criminals out of the precious parks and plazas that New Yorkers rely on for recreation and relaxation. They freed precinct commanders to deal directly, and on their own initiative, with neighborhood matters such as prostitution and liquor sales to minors. Instead of waiting for city agents from the Department of Environmental Protection or Department of Motor Vehicles to enforce laws against custom-tooled cars with outsized speakers booming music at deafening volume or against straight-piped motorcycles, local officers could make citations and seize illegally modified vehicles on the spot.

Strategy No. 5 also curtailed the use of summonses and "desk appearance tickets" (DATs) to deal with "low-level" crimes. People caught drinking alcohol in public or hanging out in parks after closing frequently just get a citation on the spot rather than a pair of handcuffs, or if they do get brought to the station, they may receive a "notice to appear" from the desk sergeant and then get released. This system is fine as far as it goes, because there is no particular reason to bring every litterer or public urinator to jail for a weekend. But the system was open to abuse, as many routine violators of public order would give fake names or throw their tickets in the trash. Even if they accrued warrants for arrest as a result of failing to appear in court, cops might not run a check on everyone they stopped. Getting DATs and summonses became a joke.

Bratton changed the rules. If someone didn't have photo ID on them to prove they were who they said they were, they were ineligible for a criminal court summons. And repeat offenders weren't eligible at all. With summonses and DATs reserved for minor violators who weren't routinely in trouble, neighborhood deviants began to consider the consequences of customary lawbreaking more seriously.

This counterintuitive, bottom-up approach began to pay dividends. In 1994, Giuliani's first year in office, murder fell by close to 20 percent; in 1995, it dropped by another 25 percent. The city began an aggressive war on street crime. Arrests of fare beaters in the subway system, begun by Bratton in 1990, wound up snaring wanted felons with outstanding warrants, as well as people illegally toting guns. Murderers and armed robbers, it seemed, were not so scrupulous about paying their fare; conveniently, policing small violations of the law caught bigger criminals, too. A net for minnows also catches bass.

But it's important to note that broken windows never meant "zero tolerance." It is not an authoritarian program to impose orderliness by force, nor is its success measured by making as many arrests as possible of anyone caught spitting on the sidewalk. As George Kelling wrote in 2019,

> The assertiveness of Broken Windows misdemeanor enforcement, however, does not equate with "zero tolerance" policies and high-arrest strategies, as is sometimes alleged; done correctly, order-maintenance policing does not rely on such practices.

Broken windows is a humane and tolerant means of restoring community control to dysfunctional neighborhoods through enhanced police presence and social course correction, building "the sense of security that citizens need in order to do their part to enforce community norms, knowing that backup is not far away," in Kelling's words.

Neighborhoods of the city like Washington Heights, bisected by Interstate 95, were destination spots for drug buyers from Virginia to Boston. The NYPD arrested dozens of local dealers in major raids and blockaded entire streets, allowing only local residents to pass. Civil libertarians howled at the strong-arm tactics, but Giuliani and Bratton's successor Howard Safir—a former federal agent with deep experience in fighting narcotics at the Drug Enforcement Agency—proved that they could make the city safer by pushing back against the scourge of drugs. "We enforce drug laws because we believe that drugs cause crime," Safir said. "We think 80 percent of the crimes in the city are tied to drugs. So the measure of our success has to be crime reduction."

Neighborhood residents welcomed the forceful intervention because their streets, formerly open-air drug markets where gangs would routinely stage gun battles over turf, became peaceful. Children could play outside, and grown-ups could stroll and chat with neighbors. Broken windows theory turned out to work. It isn't so much that every graffiti writer, turnstile-jumper, gambler, or even drug dealer is dangerously violent but that their presence indicates an anything-goes environment that law-abiding people—always the vast majority of any neighborhood—find frightening. This fear of crime inhibits participation in the community, which means less quality of life.

But even more important than neighborhood policing and enforcement of QoL offenses, Bill Bratton's adoption of the CompStat system truly revolutionized policing and the culture of the NYPD in a way that sets the CompStat era truly apart from what came before. Originating in a set of maps that a transit police lieutenant marked with pins to designate robberies in the subway system, CompStat evolved into a data-heavy method of tracking crime and crime trends on a granular level. Precinct commanders were given added freedom to strategize crime fighting in their districts but were held strictly accountable for failure to reduce complaints and make arrests. Weekly CompStat meetings surveyed the state of crime and minutely measured the progress that was made on an ongoing basis.

Writing in 1999, Bratton described his public strategy.

As part of the quality-of-life initiative, the police checked identification of people stopped for minor offenses. When the checks turned up a wanted person, a parole violator, or a repeat offender, cops arrested and searched him, instead of letting him off with a relatively toothless desk-appearance ticket, as is usual with minor offenders.

This intensified police presence had an almost immediate impact on illegal guns. We flooded shooting hot spots, identified through the CompStat maps, with both uniformed and plainclothes enforcement teams. People carrying illegal guns quickly realized that they risked gun charges after being arrested for minor crimes. After rising briefly in 1994, gun apprehensions then began to fall; the gunslingers were leaving their weapons at home.

By the end of Rudy Giuliani's second term in office in 2001, New York City marked 649 murders (not counting the exogenous fatalities associated with the 9/11 attacks), a 67 percent drop from 1993, the year he was elected. From 1994 to 1997, the NYPD seized more than 56,000 guns as a result of its strong street presence and enforcement of the law. Giuliani's aggressive approach to law and order, which is now ridiculed and dismissed as cryptofascism, was an undeniable success. Giuliani's policies quite literally saved thousands of lives and helped turn America's greatest city from a disastrous course toward capital flight and impoverishment.

September 11, 2001, was primary day in New York City for the election to replace Giuliani, who was term limited. In the wake of the al-Qaida terror attacks, the election was moved up two weeks, but more significantly, New Yorkers rallied around the man who became known as "America's Mayor." Giuliani, whom many New Yorkers had tired of after eight years of his abrasive personality, regained his credibility, and his support for Republican candidate Michael Bloomberg is largely credited with pushing the billionaire over the finish line to win narrowly against Democrat Mark Green. Curiously, Bernhard Goetz also ran for mayor in 2001, on the Fusion ticket, garnering some 1,049 votes.

Mike Bloomberg took over City Hall at a grim moment in New York City history. The "pit" of the former Twin Towers was still a smoking mess where more than 2,600 people had been killed, and many believed that New York would never come back. Ten percent of the city's workers lost their jobs, and 18,000 small and local enterprises went out of business. Tourism dropped off sharply. Lower Manhattan, the center of the national financial industry, almost seemed like a write-off, with experts predicting that banks and other firms would relocate into less dense and more secure areas.

Pursuing vigorous pro-growth policies, Bloomberg kept the financial industry intact downtown and also pushed to diversify the municipal economy into technology, health, and education. He also noted the impressive crime numbers of his predecessor and vowed to continue progress toward making the city even safer. He hired Ray Kelly as police commissioner. Kelly, who had run the NYPD in Dinkins' final 15 months in office, was credited with effective outreach to black churches and increasing minority officer recruitment. It was Kelly who had instituted the "Safe Streets, Safe City" program, a community policing initiative that put thousands more cops in high-crime neighborhoods.

Kelly became the first NYPD commissioner to come back to the job, and he and Bloomberg resolved to continue the work that had begun under Giuliani. But with the murder rate already down to its mid-60s levels, additional declines would be hard fought. The solution they pursued was to get guns off the street by intensifying the practice of "stop, question, and frisk" (SQF) that had already been under wide use in the previous administration.

SQF is a constitutionally protected practice, ratified by the Supreme Court in the 1968 *Terry v. Ohio* decision, that permits police to stop and question people under reasonable suspicion of committing a crime, and to frisk them to see if they have a weapon, for the safety of the officer during the interaction. Kelly expanded the use of the tactic. In 2002, the first year of Bloomberg's mayoralty, there were around 97,000 recorded stops; by 2011, the NYPD made about 685,000 stops. About half of these stops were followed by a "protective frisk." The murder rate continued to fall, and by 2013, the last year of the Bloomberg administration, there were only 332 murders, or fewer than one per day, a frequency that had not been seen since 1958.

The practice garnered a lot of criticism—and a major federal lawsuit—from activists who insisted it was racially motivated. And it's true that 52 percent of all the people stopped between 2004 and 2012 were black, while blacks in 2010 comprised only 23 percent of New York's population. But the police said they were never driven to stop people based on race and that they simply went where the crime was.

This is the same argument that is going on today when we hear about the supposedly disproportionate use of force by police forces around the country against black people, and the same counterargument is made in return: black people commit a disproportionate amount of violent crime and thus have a higher rate of police interactions.

Indeed, violent crime in New York City is heavily concentrated among blacks. In 2010, blacks were the suspect in 60 percent of all murders and 74 percent of all shootings. In 2019, blacks were the suspect in 51 percent of all murders and 74 percent of all shootings, though they comprise less than a quarter of the population. These numbers, especially for gun crimes, remain remarkably consistent across time. If you want to fight crime and get illegal guns off the street, you are going to wind up in neighborhoods that are largely black.

A class-action lawsuit against New York City and the police department to end its use of SQF, on the basis of racial discrimination, was launched in 2008. The case was tried before Shira Scheindlin, a radical activist judge who signaled her contempt for the city's position throughout the proceedings. Judge Scheindlin found for the plaintiffs and imposed a battery of reforms on the NYPD, including independent oversight.

Scheindlin pointed out that relatively few guns were actually seized as a result of frisking people. "A weapon was found after 1.5% of these frisks. In other words, in 98.5% of the 2.3 million frisks, no weapon was found." Finding 35,000 illegal weapons being carried by suspicious characters isn't nothing, but what's also important to consider is all the weapons that were left at home because their owners knew there was a good chance they would get busted for carrying them. Not finding weapons can be as good as finding them if the goal is to limit the extent to which they are used to cause harm.

The city under Bloomberg appealed Scheindlin's ruling, and the higher court not only stayed the reforms that Scheindlin imposed but sent the case down to be handled by a different judge. Scheindlin, the circuit court found, not only had inappropriately arranged to try the case in the first place but gave interviews about the case while it was going on and made remarks that indicated her prejudice toward the plaintiffs.

Among Bill de Blasio's first acts as mayor, the same month he was sworn in, was to give up the city's appeal of the SQF case and to begin to fulfill his campaign promises of sweeping public safety reforms. Because of the new mayor's capitulation, the NYPD was placed under a federal monitor. Twenty years of the nation's most successful experiment in fighting crime were now at an end, and a radical Progressive Democrat was in charge of New York's police.

· · · · · · · · · ·

Following the death of Eric Garner, tensions were running high in New York City, and Mayor de Blasio did little to ease them. Two weeks after Garner died, the mayor convened a round table on police-community relations. The mayor, naturally enough, was seated at the main table, flanked by NYPD Commissioner Bratton and, to the surprise of many,

Al Sharpton. Sharpton, a close de Blasio ally, has been an outspoken critic of the police for decades, and his presence in such a significant position imparted the distinct impression that in the hierarchy of the de Blasio administration, he was a coeval figure to the police commissioner.

There are few characters in New York City over the last 40 years who have been as consistently divisive and inflammatory as Al Sharpton. He gained national prominence as the primary proponent of the Tawana Brawley rape hoax in 1987, when a 15-year-old black girl in the Hudson Valley north of New York City fabricated a kidnapping and assault. Brawley, under Sharpton's apparent direction, named the local district attorney and a number of local police officers as her assailants. The case—which was manifestly false—fell apart, and Sharpton was sued for defamation; he refused to pay the six-figure judgment, which was eventually settled by a group of prominent black businessmen.

In 1991, Sharpton inserted himself into the Crown Heights riot, which was the largest sustained anti-Semitic attack in American history. Sparked when a car driven by a Hasidic Jew jumped the curb and killed Gavin Cato, a black boy, the riot continued for days. Jews were beaten in the streets, Jewish-owned stores were looted, and Jewish homes were attacked with stones. Over 150 police officers were injured, and a rabbinical student was stabbed to death.

Sharpton gave a eulogy at Gavin Cato's funeral, at which he criticized Jews for selling diamonds from apartheid South Africa; a banner reading "Hitler Did Not Do the Job" was hoisted in the crowd. The next day, Sharpton announced, "If the Jews want to get it on, tell them to pin their yarmulkes back and come over to my house." On the third day of the riot, when Mayor David Dinkins was begging for peace, Sharpton led a march through Crown Heights; an Israeli flag was burned.

In 1995, Sharpton led a protest in Harlem against a Jewish commercial tenant who, at the request of his black landlord, was evicting a black subtenant. Sharpton inveighed against "white interlopers." Afterward, one of the protestors entered the store, shot several people, and set it on fire. Eight people, including the killer, died. Sharpton disavowed any responsibility for the incident.

Sharpton's repulsive history of advocacy is long and unvaried. In 2008, he flew to West Palm Beach, Florida, to protest the treatment of four black teens who had been arrested for rape. It was unfair, Sharpton said, that the men were not released on bail, when some white suspects had received allegedly softer treatment. The youths he made a point of defending had beaten and raped a Haitian woman and forced her at gunpoint to have sex with her own son.

De Blasio's affection and enthusiasm for Sharpton were amplified by the displeasure they caused his critics. At Sharpton's sixtieth birthday party in 2014, de Blasio's love for "the Rev" spilled over. He gushed

And the more people criticize him, the more I want to hang out with him. Because a lot of times, just look who's doing the criticizing and the way they're saying it—it makes you realize the Rev must be doing something right. You know, sometimes, your enemies are the best endorsers of the righteousness of your actions.

"The more people criticize him, the more I want to hang out with him." This is a curious thing to say, and it speaks to an immature, reactive part of de Blasio's personality, which colored his entire administration. Anything that bothers one of his "enemies" vindicates his actions, and as a political creature, anyone who opposes him is an enemy. Therefore, the angrier he makes people, the more he knows he is doing the right thing.

The image of the mayor sitting between Bill Bratton and Al Sharpton at a forum on police-community relations sent rank-and-file cops—as well as ordinary New Yorkers—a clear message that the divisive firebrand had equal say as the head of the police when it came to how City Hall would deal with questions of public safety. And Sharpton made the most of the opportunity, lambasting both the mayor and the commissioner over the death of Eric Garner, casting it starkly as a racially motivated murder.

> Given the data that we are seeing in terms of these Broken Window kind of operations, it's disproportionate in the black and Latino community. If Dante wasn't your son, he'd been candidate for a chokehold. And we've got to deal with that reality.

Sharpton's invocation of the mayor's son personalized a public forum that was intended to cool the climate of roiling animosity and raised the heat and stakes of the conversation considerably. He then turned to Bratton and roasted him, too.

I heard the commissioner say race wasn't involved. We don't know that. How do we assume before an investigation that a policeman with two civil rights violations didn't have race involved? So we gon' prejudge what we want and tell the community to wait on the results?

Following this disastrous "community roundtable," the impression garnered by everyone was that Sharpton had cornered the mayor and the commissioner. As an invited guest, Sharpton could speak his mind; as high city officials, de Blasio and Bratton had to hold their tongues. In the eyes of the public, especially among cops, the mayor got played.

In December of 2014, a Staten Island grand jury refused to return an indictment on Officer Pantaleo in the death of Eric Garner. At a somber press conference held that evening, de Blasio, surrounded by African American city councilmembers and other dignitaries, repeated almost verbatim Sharpton's words from a few months before. "Chirlane and I have had to talk to Dante for years, about the dangers he may face," he explained, referencing his mixed-race son, whom he characterized as "a good young man, a law-abiding young man, who would never think to do anything wrong." De Blasio continued

Yet, because of a history that still hangs over us, the dangers he may face—we've had to literally train him, as families have all over this city for decades, in how to take special care in any encounter he has with the police officers who are there to protect him. . . . So I've had to worry, over the years, Chirlane's had to worry—was Dante safe each night?

Drawing a comparison between Eric Garner and Dante de Blasio was tendentious and grotesque. Eric Garner was a middle-aged career criminal who died while resisting arrest for selling untaxed cigarettes while on bail for multiple offenses. The mayor's son, at the time, was a Yale-bound honor student who presumably understood the basic rules of not being a serial petty criminal or mouthing off to cops when they spoke to him and not to resist arrest.

The theme of "the Talk" that parents of black boys are required to have with their sons—not to resist arrest and to follow officers' orders—is commonly bemoaned as a burden that blacks uniquely have to bear in the face of constant police harassment, a sad but necessary rite of passage. Yet it's clear in the cases of Eric Garner, George Floyd, Mike Brown, and Jacob Blake that they never got the Talk, or if they did, it didn't take. Shootings of black men by the police are not disproportionate to their share of the population when the higher rate of black criminality is factored in. And the number of unarmed black men who die annually at the hands of the police can normally be counted on one's fingers.

The insinuation that Dante de Blasio was in danger from "the police officers who are there to protect him" had a special meaning because the de Blasio family literally was protected, night and day, by highly trained NYPD detectives. The suggestion that the mayor's own security detail might, at any moment, murder a member of his family out of racial hostility was seen as a general slur against the police.

Tensions escalated a few days later, after protestors attacked cops on the Brooklyn Bridge during an anti-police march. Eric Linsker, a poet and adjunct professor in the city university system, dropped a garbage can on two police lieutenants. Other protestors punched cops as they tried to arrest Linsker; one of the assailants, Jarrod Shanahan, is now a college professor in Illinois, and he is cited in the *New York Times* and other esteemed publications as an expert on criminal justice theory and Rikers Island in particular. Mayor de Blasio spoke of the violence against the police—which resulted in a broken nose and other injuries—as "alleged."

But it was a few weeks after telling the world that he considered New York's Finest as potential assassins of his own child that tensions between the mayor and the police exploded and an irreparable fission of trust was formed that persists today. On December 20, 2014, Ismaaiyl Abdullah Brinsley boarded a bus in Baltimore with a savage mission. Earlier in the day he threatened to kill himself in front of his ex-girlfriend; she managed to talk him out of it, only to have him turn his gun on her, wounding her badly with a shot to the abdomen.

Brinsley posted on social media his plan to kill cops in revenge for the deaths of Eric Garner and Mike Brown earlier that year. "I'm putting Wings on Pigs today," he alerted his Instagram followers. "They take 1 of ours. . . . Lets [*sic*] take 2 of Theirs." When he arrived in Brooklyn, he went looking for targets and quickly found them. Rafael Ramos and Wenjian Liu, uniformed NYPD officers, were sitting in their patrol car on Myrtle Avenue in the Bed-Stuy neighborhood. Brinsley fired four shots at the officers through the open window of their cruiser, hitting them in the head and chest and killing them instantly. He then fled into a nearby subway station and killed himself.

Police were aggrieved and outraged, which is customary when officers die in the line of duty. But in this case their anger was directed at Mayor de Blasio, whom they felt had put a target on their back—first by giving Al Sharpton a prominent role as an advisor on race and policing and more specifically by sanctifying the death of Eric Garner and drawing a tight comparison between him and his own child. The night of the shootings, de Blasio went to the hospital where the officers' bodies were cooling, and many cops turned their backs to him; he approached some members of the force to express his sympathies and was rebuffed.

Pat Lynch, head of the Patrolmen's Benevolent Association, ripped the mayor, saying

There's blood on many hands tonight. Those that incited violence on the streets under the guise of protest that tried to tear down what NYPD officers did every day. We tried to warn it must not go on, it cannot be tolerated. That blood on the hands starts at City Hall in the office of the mayor.

The Sergeants Benevolent Association Twitter account proclaimed, "The blood of 2 executed police officers is on the hands of Mayor de Blasio."

More than 20,000 officers attended the funeral of Rafael Ramos, and many of them turned their backs on the mayor when he spoke; the same happened a week later at the funeral of Wenjian Liu. Cops across the city felt sold out by the mayor. "The mayor has no respect for us," Camille Sanfilippo, a retired NYPD detective, told a reporter. "Why should we have respect for him?"

Following the funerals of officers Liu and Ramos, the NYPD initiated a minor labor stoppage in the form of a slowdown of arrests for minor crimes. The results were alarming, as the criminal element roused itself and crime went up. De Blasio recognized that his relationship with the NYPD—at least among the rank and file—had been damaged. He moved his relationship with Al Sharpton out of the spotlight and adopted language of support for the police— in word at least, if not always in deed.

De Blasio continued to make missteps. In the early morning of July 5, 2017, as Independence Day celebrations were winding down, NYPD officer Miosotis Familia—a 12-year veteran of the force and mother of three—was murdered on duty as she sat in a mobile command post. Her assassin, Alexander Bonds, had a long history of admission to jail and mental hospitals and had expressed hostility toward the police on social media. Bonds was killed by pursuing officers after he pointed his gun at them.

The mayor raised eyebrows when less than 36 hours after the killing of Familia he skipped an NYPD swearing-in ceremony and jetted off to Germany to attend a protest against a meeting of the G-20, attended by President Trump and other world leaders. The protest, called *Hamburg Zeigt Haltung*, or "Hamburg Shows Attitude," spotlighted democratic resistance to global capitalism; it was attended by riots, arson, and looting.

Though he returned to the United States in time for Officer Familia's funeral, de Blasio's attendance at a leftist rally in Hamburg struck many New Yorkers as somewhat bizarre, if not disrespectful. His pointless, anodyne comments ("And how will we stop the curse of climate change? We'll stop it in Hamburg, we will stop it in New York City, and cities and towns all over the world. We will make the difference.") caused observers to wonder if de Blasio—who was, after all, running for reelection just a few months later—was really so interested in being mayor of America's largest and most complicated city. Or did he have his eye focused on bigger things?

In any case, the murders of Ramos and Liu by Ismaaiyl Brinsley took place near the beginning of the first cycle of protests, riots, and violence associated with the Black Lives Matter movement. BLM was formed after the July 2013 acquittal of George Zimmerman in his murder trial for the killing of Trayvon Martin but really took off as a national force following Michael Brown's shooting death in Ferguson, Missouri, in August 2014. The anti-police sentiment that spread across the country had a rebound consequence on policing and crime that has been identified as the "Ferguson effect."

The Ferguson effect, which has since been documented and validated, is a reaction by police, following a period of intense criticism, where they become much less proactive in their crime-fighting posture. It's not a slowdown, or "blue flu," so much as a defensive response to heightened scrutiny and the assumption of a reactive position vis-à-vis crime.

There's nothing easier than to take a cellphone video of a contentious interaction between a cop and a civilian in a heated, crowded situation, crop it to make it look abusive, and drop it on social media to stir up a mob. Misleading videos can have harmful effects. In August 2020, just as the hysteria around the death of George Floyd was sputtering out, police in Kenosha, Wisconsin, shot a man, Jacob Blake, who was reaching into his car for a knife. Video from an obstructed view went viral, sparking another round of riots and violence around the country.

As police retreat from proactive engagement with the community in order to prevent crime, malefactors are emboldened to carry weapons, hang out with known associates, ramp up rather than suppress quarrels and beefs, and commit crimes. As police release pressure, criminals respond quickly; no one is more attuned to the nuances of police presence than lawbreakers. This dynamic occurred in the two years following the Ferguson riots in cities around the country, as evidenced by fewer arrests and soaring murder rates in St. Louis, Chicago, Washington, DC, Baltimore, and Milwaukee.

New York City experienced a small but significant 8 percent rise in homicides in 2015, but murders dropped off in the following years. The control that New York demonstrated over crime helped reinforce the theme that New York is "the safest big city in the nation," as de Blasio repeated virtually anytime the topic of crime was raised. Critics of the de Blasio program of reform, starting with the end of SQF, cautioned that he was setting the scene for an unwinding of the city's carefully constructed and maintained civic safety. When murders and crime stayed low or declined, de Blasio applauded himself, derided his critics, and swore that he had unlocked a new recipe for just policing in New York.

Making things worse, at the end of 2017, the city council passed and the mayor signed a set of bills called the "Right to Know Act." Unsatisfied with the extent to which limiting

stop-and-frisk had restrained police from investigating suspicious persons and getting guns off the street, the Right to
Know Act, in the words of one of its sponsors, "regulates the
day-to-day street encounters between police and civilians."
One stipulation of the act requires officers to hand out business cards to virtually anyone they question and provide a
reason for initiating law enforcement activity. This rule was
designed to interfere operationally with police work, and
thereby limit interactions, in the name of transparency.

The other, more significant aspect of the Right to Know
Act has a far more chilling effect on investigative police
work and basically handcuffs cops. The Supreme Court, in
a series of important Fourth Amendment cases, has carefully laid out the rules of police searches in such a way
that people may be secure against "unreasonable searches
and seizures." As such, police are required to get consent
to conduct searches that fall outside of specific cases con-
cerning the immediate safety of the officer. Getting consent
can be achieved simply by asking a suspect to empty his or
her pockets or open his or her backpack; the courts have
allowed that a certain amount of indirection on the part of
the police is permitted and that individuals are responsible for understanding that giving consent effectively waives
their constitutional rights.

New York City's Right to Know Act includes a provision
mandating informed consent. The officer is required proac-
tively to inform people that they are not required to consent
to a search. A few other jurisdictions have informed consent
laws regarding traffic stops, in an effort to counter racial
profiling. But no other place demands that cops make clear,

using plain and simple language delivered in a nonthreaten-
ing manner, that the person who is the subject of the search
is being asked to voluntarily, knowingly, and intelligently
consent to such search, and explaining that such search will
not be conducted if such person refuses to provide consent
to such search.

This isn't just a chilling effect—it's a deep freeze, zero Kelvin,
essentially making basic police work impossible by forcing
cops to act as impromptu legal aid interpreters for the suspects they are trying to investigate.

In January 2018, the mayor spoke at a tribute to Martin
Luther King, Jr., at the Brooklyn Academy of Music. He
celebrated the movement against "a broken and unconsti-
tutional policy of stop-and-frisk," despite "the voices of the
status quo," who said, "there was no room for change, there
was no possibility." The fight for change, led by himself and
a mobilized group of activists, led to "a policy of neighborhood policing, and guess what, because we got fairer, we are
the safest big city in America. We proved with a whole city
watching but also the whole country watching that safety
and fairness could walk hand-in-hand."

It's hard to say that de Blasio was totally wrong, because
crime was largely kept in check for the first years of his
reforms. The mayor and his backers in government, academia, and the media ran a lot of victory laps while chuck-
ling at the stop-and-frisk bitter-enders and die-hards who
wagged their fingers and warned that the fabric of public
order was showing signs of wear. But a plausible case can
be made—and recent trends bear it out—that the positive

changes that broken windows policing made in New York over the 20 years before de Blasio took office were so profound and significant that unwinding them would require concerted effort. Entropy doesn't happen overnight; it's a gradual process that occurs over years of neglect and decay.

The great Scottish economist and philosopher Adam Smith, responding to the news in 1777 that George Washington had defeated the British forces at Saratoga, assured his panicked friend, "There is a great deal of ruin in a nation." Smith meant that great nations can't be destroyed all at once: a responsible government insures itself against degradation by shoring up its timbers, keeping its books in order, and pruning weeds and clearing dead wood. The same thing can be said about New York City. Twenty years of good civic habits, and all their collateral benefits in the form of a higher tax base and better opportunities, can't be undone all at once. There is a great deal of ruin in a city, too. But de Blasio and his radical machine did their utmost, from the beginning, to spread the rot.

3

New Crime City: Savage Permission

O N JUNE 1, 2018, someone at the Fort Hamilton Army Garrison in Brooklyn ordered a pizza. Fort Hamilton, located in Bay Ridge, near the Verrazano-Narrows Bridge, is the only active Department of Defense installation in New York City. The pizzeria, located in Queens (it's unclear, by the way, why anyone at Fort Hamilton decided to call Queens for a pizza, when Fort Hamilton is located between Bay Ridge and Bensonhurst, basically the Pizza Belt of Brooklyn), sent its deliveryman, Pablo Villavicencio, to drive the pizza to the base. When he got there, he was asked to show his driver's license—standard when entering any government building, much less a military garrison.

But Villavicencio, an illegal immigrant from Ecuador, had no driver's license and offered the guard his NYC municipal ID card instead—though he resided outside the city in Nassau County. The guard ran a security check—standard operating procedure for anyone trying to enter the base—and discovered that Villavicencio had an open order of deportation dating to 2010. The base took him into custody and turned him over to Immigration and Customs Enforcement (ICE).

New York's class of professional advocates and elected officials exploded with rage and rushed into action to defend their new martyr. Hundreds of people staged a march to the gate of the base, chanting their perennial slogan, "No hate! No fear! Immigrants are welcome here!" Protesters stood in the street linking arms to block traffic; seven were arrested. Others used empty pizza boxes as placards to demonstrate support. "Free Pablo!" some read. "A father has been taken from his family!" Villavicencio's wife and small daughters figured at the forefront of media coverage; his family wept and begged for his release.

Governor Andrew Cuomo weighed in, invoking the presence of the Statue of Liberty in nearby New York Harbor. "The detention of Pablo Villavicencio as he was delivering pizza at Fort Hamilton—under the gaze of Lady Liberty— goes against everything we believe in," pronounced Cuomo, though he failed to explain just what "beliefs" or core principles were violated when the guard at a federal installation called the authorities after Villavicencio turned out to have an open order of deportation.

Cuomo extended an offer of free legal assistance to Villavicencio and his family, "though the Liberty Defense

Project, which is the nation's first state-led project to assist immigrants, regardless of status, in obtaining access to legal services." Mayor de Blasio chimed in, too, averring, "Delivering a pizza is not a threat to public safety. The ultimate city of immigrants stands ready to provide him and his family with any assistance we can."

Delivering a pizza as an activity in itself may not be "a threat to public safety," but surely it is a problem when a driver has no license and presumably no insurance. Villavicencio was held by ICE for 53 days before a judge ordered his release, to great applause from his defenders. A few months later, however, Pablo Villavicencio was back in the news, when he was arrested for beating up his wife and taking her cell phone.

Pablo appears not to have faced any major consequences from abusing his spouse, though they do seem to have split up. His experiences, if anything, have encouraged his sense of indignation about how unfair American society is. On his Facebook page, he left a series of comments after George Floyd's death. "Full video of the assassination of an African American by a white extremist policeman, whose hatred for all minorities was fed by President Trump," he wrote. Having been told he was a victim of racism, he is now an ardent exponent of wokeness regarding life in America, the Land of the Damned.

The case of Pablo Villavicencio might seem odd: why would New York's political elite rush to defend the honor of a criminal alien, not even a resident of the city, arrested in a perfectly normal course of events as he tried to enter an army base? Part of the answer is, of course, the Democratic sanctification of illegal aliens following the rise of Donald Trump. But New York's elevation of illegal immigrants as a special class predates Trump and is part of the general trend toward dismantling the rule of law.

The fight to end SQF was only a first step in the Progressive ascension to power, which not only elevated Bill de Blasio to the mayoralty but also saw hard-left politicians take over many functions in government. In his first term, de Blasio installed Melissa Mark-Viverito as speaker of the city council to serve as his legislative cat's paw. Mark-Viverito, originally from Puerto Rico, is a hardcore partisan for illegal aliens and a fervent supporter of long-imprisoned terrorist Oscar López Rivera, whose Fuerzas Armadas por la Liberación Nacional (FALN) waged a deadly bombing campaign around the United States in the 1970s.

The city council under Progressive direction began to act steadily to reduce the authority and jurisdiction of the police and erode public safety in New York. In 2014, just seven months into de Blasio's first term, the council passed a bill banning federal immigration authorities from Rikers Island, the city's jail complex, and ended virtually all cooperation between the city's Department of Corrections and ICE.

New York City is famously a "city of immigrants," and millions of newcomers entered the country through Ellis Island, the nation's primary immigration inspection center, between 1892 and 1954. Even today, approximately 35 percent of New York's population was born in another country. Immigrants come to New York to pursue the classic dream of improving their station in life, and by and large they are a net benefit to the city and the country as a whole.

Most of the immigrants in New York City are here under color of law, either as citizens, legal permanent residents, or holding another visa status. It is estimated that about 500,000 illegal aliens reside in New York. Many of these "undocumented immigrants" work either "under the table," for cash, or with forged or stolen documents and Social Security numbers, which can be readily purchased for a few hundred dollars in immigrant neighborhoods. But—fraud and identity theft aside—even most illegal aliens are generally law-abiding.

Under Giuliani, New York adopted a "sanctuary" policy to accommodate the reality of the situation that between 4 and 7 percent of the population was illegally present in the country and that many households were of "mixed status," with some members here legally and others not. Sanctuary was a kind of "don't ask, don't tell" regime whereby city services such as schools, hospitals, and the police didn't enquire about immigration status. This system made sense insofar as detectives wanted illegal immigrants not to feel anxious about reporting crimes or serving as witnesses, public health officials didn't want diseased illegals spreading infection, and the city generally didn't want children not to attend school just because they or their parents were undocumented.

However, the city openly cooperated with immigration enforcement, especially when it came to sharing information about noncitizens—legal or illegal—who were criminals. Even legal permanent residents, "green card holders" who are allowed to work and travel freely, can be deported if they commit crimes. And New York City was always aggressive about helping find and deport foreigners who failed to respect our laws. Following 9/11, Mike Bloomberg and Ray Kelly solidified agreements with the feds, including cooperation between ICE and the Department of Corrections, which would, upon request, detain criminal aliens for federal immigration authorities to take into custody and process for deportation. Wanted criminals and felons, many of whom had been previously removed from the country, were taken into custody and deported to their home nations.

Under de Blasio and Mark-Viverito, the Progressive regime quickly moved to undo the agreement between New York and ICE. The federal authorities were kicked off of Rikers Island, and the city refused to honor so-called detainer requests, unless they pertained to aliens who had been convicted of extraordinarily serious crimes, but only within the last five years and if the request was accompanied by a judicial warrant. Mayor de Blasio proclaimed frequently that "170 crimes" of an especially heinous nature were exempted from the noncooperation protocol, though sexual misconduct, forcible touching, sexual abuse in the second or third degree, grand larceny, and welfare fraud were not among them. These, according to the mayor, were among the "very minor crimes" that would not merit deportation.

When asked why the NYPD would be barred from cooperating with ICE in deporting someone who was caught and convicted of driving drunk, de Blasio had no problem in excusing the behavior. "Drunk driving that does not lead to any other negative outcome, I could define as [a very minor offense]," he told CNN. Of course, the problem is that people who experience a "negative outcome"—such as killing someone while driving drunk—have typically done it before. The point of imposing serious consequences on drunk drivers is to stop them from doing it in the first place.

When the law was eventually amended to include "patronizing a minor for prostitution, patronizing a person for prostitution in a school zone, and sex trafficking of a child" as crimes that could merit deportation, many prominent activists were horrified—not that these crimes had been originally omitted but that de Blasio was deepening cooperation between the NYPD and ICE. Javier Valdés, an executive with Make the Road, a radical activist organization that receives around $10 million annually in city and state funding, said it was "deeply disturbing" that convicted sex traffickers could now face detention by federal immigration authorities. "The mayor must reverse course, and all other current elected officials and candidates looking to lead our city in the future should make clear that this is unacceptable," harrumphed Valdés, scolding de Blasio.

The law technically permits the NYPD and the Department of Corrections to turn individuals listed on the national terrorist watch list over to the federal authorities. But even when it comes to terrorists, the city can detain them only for a short period of time,

> provided, however, that if federal immigration authorities fail to present the department with a judicial warrant for such person within the period described above, such person shall be released and the department shall not notify federal immigration authorities of such person's release.

So if the feds don't get the paperwork in quickly enough, the city is obligated to release the suspected terrorist—and can't even inform ICE that they had the suspect and let him or her go.

New York is a sanctuary city for illegal aliens, though everyone else remains at their tender mercies. "Sanctuary," despite its overtones of refuge and asylum, is not a benign policy, as 92-year-old Maria Fuertes found out. A legal immigrant from the Dominican Republic who had lived in New York for more than 50 years, Fuertes was a mother and grandmother who kept to herself, took care of stray cats, and picked up cans around her Queens neighborhood to return for pocket change.

In January of 2020, Maria Fuertes was raped by 21-year-old Reeaz Khan, an illegal alien from Guyana. She was found lying in the street in freezing weather. Her spine was broken, her ribs were cracked, and she had internal injuries consistent with sexual assault. She died in the hospital.

Khan had been arrested just six weeks earlier for beating up his father and putting him in the hospital. When ICE realized Khan was in the country illegally, the agency issued a detainer and asked the NYPD to hold him until they could pick him up; the NYPD declined the request, and Khan was released—without bail—the same day.

The case garnered national attention when the acting chief of ICE blamed the sanctuary policies of New York City for the murder of Fuertes. And at her funeral, her son, Hugo Fuertes, agreed: "I blame the city. . . . He was a criminal and they did not pay attention to this. They left him in the streets and he continued to do his misdeeds—because of that my mother is dead."

Asked to comment, Mayor de Blasio spoke angrily—about Donald Trump.

> The problem I have here is there's an effort being made to politicize this situation, to take a policy which is actually meant to protect people and has protected people—we are the safest big city in America because of policies like this—and use it as fodder for what is nothing less than a political effort by ICE.

De Blasio then spoke up on behalf of Reeaz Khan, noting that he was technically innocent of beating, slashing, and hospitalizing his father at the time he raped and killed Maria Fuertes.

> We say there are 170 serious crimes—violent crimes—if you are convicted of any of those, you should be deported at that point. We will work with ICE at that point. But you have to be convicted. There has to be an actual legal process that leads somewhere. In this instance, the individual was never convicted, I'm not sure there even was a trial.... [W]e have to have a standard that stops ICE from taking anybody, anytime, for anything, and literally tearing a family apart, depriving a family typically of the breadwinner, leaving the rest here with us, with no means of support.

It is striking how Mayor de Blasio transitions here from talking about a specific case to painting a general picture of hardworking "undocumented immigrants" who are supporting a family. But Reeaz Khan had no children and worked sporadically and illegally as a day laborer. He was not a breadwinner. His own brother turned him in when he recognized Khan on a police alert. The only family that was torn apart, as opposed to de Blasio's imaginary case, was the Fuertes family, which had to bury its matriarch after she was raped and left to die next to a pile of garbage bags.

Reeaz Khan is an especially egregious case, but he is hardly the only example of an illegal alien criminal whom ICE tried to deport, only to be stymied by the dictates of a Progressive political apparatus that is reflexively and ideologically opposed to the enforcement of immigration law. According to ICE, the agency submitted more than 7,500 detainer requests to the NYPD, the Department of Corrections, and Westchester County over the course of the 2018–2019 fiscal year. Virtually all the requests were denied, meaning that the law enforcement agencies already had criminal illegal aliens in custody and were informed that they were wanted for deportation, and they released them anyway.

These illegal aliens accounted for almost 18,000 prior criminal convictions, in addition to 6,500 new criminal charges. Their crimes included 200 homicides, more than 1,000 sexual offenses, 3,500 assaults, and more than 1,500 drunk driving convictions. Advocates for illegal aliens and sanctuary city policies always claim that immigrants have a lower rate of crime than the native-born population, and there is merit to this claim—especially if you lump together legal and illegal immigrants. But the real point is that immigrants ought to commit no crime. We should expect more, not less, of guests and newcomers who wanted to come here.

Ending cooperation with the federal government on the deportation of aliens who had been convicted of serious crimes was a major step in de Blasio's unwinding of public order. New York has been a sanctuary city for decades. But it was de Blasio who embraced that designation to mean that the city was now a place where people who had fled their homelands for God knows what reason could commit crimes, hide out, and obtain taxpayer-funded lawyers if they got arrested. Disrespect for law and order flowed downward from de Blasio's City Hall, and his war against ICE was a major step in the process of dissolution.

· · · · · · · · · ·

Calls in 2020 to "Defund the Police" did not emerge out of nowhere. The seeds of this anarchist program were planted years before and lovingly nurtured in liberal think tanks, foundations, academia, and among hard-left political organizers, operatives, and officials. Couched in respectable, reformist language palatable to the well-meaning and well-heeled donor class, advocates who ultimately support elimination of law enforcement and prison abolition began initially by calling for reasonable-sounding proposals: fewer police stops, diversion programs even for weapons charges, reenvisioning cash bail, the release of "nonviolent" prisoners. But this path was tended by hardcore anti-police radicals from the "civil rights" complex or the defense bar, and these committed activists—as we have now seen—had firm ideas where our blind steps would lead.

A major attack on public order in New York City was the effective decriminalization of "minor crimes," including public drinking, turnstile jumping, marijuana possession, and public urination. This battle was waged both by Mayor de Blasio and his allies in the city council. In conjunction with the NYPD, de Blasio set new policies regarding discretionary enforcement. For instance, in 2014, he announced that the "simple possession" of fewer than 25 grams of marijuana would not, in most cases, result in an arrest; "burning" marijuana would continue to be an arrestable offense. However, as invariably happens whenever a behavior is depenalized, it is implicitly permitted, as are adjacent behaviors. If possessing marijuana becomes de facto legal, then smoking it becomes de facto tolerated.

In 2016, the city council passed its Criminal Justice Reform Act, a bundle of legislation that broadened the possible penalties for committing QoL offenses. The authors of the legislation recognized that few people were arrested for peeing or drinking in public, but they offered an argument that any interaction with law enforcement necessarily sets off a kind of cascade effect, resulting in the snaring of primarily nonwhite people in the bog of the criminal justice system.

The cascade argument works something like this: you live in a minority neighborhood, so you are overpoliced; you drop a candy wrapper on the ground and get a criminal summons; you don't make your court date because you have to go to class, so you get a warrant for your arrest; then you get caught in the park after sunset, and a search reveals the warrant. You go to jail on Rikers Island to wait to see the judge, and while there, you lose your job. Soon you have no choice but to join a gang and enter a life of crime and eventually wind up in prison as a hardened criminal, all because you threw a candy wrapper on the ground in an unfair system that is designed to police young men of color.

This exposition sounds compressed and absurd, but it follows the logic of anti–broken windows advocates, opponents of incarceration, and police abolitionists. The institutions of society, according to the radical left, are racist in design and operation; police, as armed agents of the state and its monopoly on violence, are the vanguard of the forces of institutional racism, attuned specifically to violations of the law by nonwhite people whose bodies the system is meant to control.

According to the theory of institutional racism, the thoughts and feelings of individual actors are irrelevant to the reality of their participation in a racist state apparatus. The good intentions of cops, teachers, or social workers do not outweigh the hundreds of years of state oppression of nonwhites. The only solution to the problem of institutional racism is to dismantle oppressive structures. But if you accept the idea that the criminal justice system is racist, then it is hard to justify any level of law enforcement, because it is all shot through with prejudicial bias, and all policing will result in disparate racial impact.

Taken to the absurd end, calling the cops on a black male is unconscionable, because there is a high likelihood that he will end up dead, another victim of racist police violence. This sounds like a strawman argument, but we hear it all the time. For instance, in late May of 2020, right before the

George Floyd incident, a white woman and a black man had a trivial argument about her unleashed dog in a quiet area of Central Park, where the man wanted to watch birds. According to his own account, Christian Cooper told Amy Cooper (no relation), "Look, if you're going to do what you want, I'm going to do what I want, but you're not going to like it"—a statement that sounds very much like a threat, no matter how you parse it.

In response, Amy Cooper told Christian Cooper, who was filming her, "I'm calling the cops. . . . I'm gonna tell them there's an African American man threatening my life." She did call 911 and reported that a black man was threatening her. It's not clear if the police ever showed up, but the pair quickly left the scene, in any event.

In an ideal world, this idiotic exchange between two high-strung neurotics would have received no comment. However, because every exchange where a white woman (a "Karen") annoys a black person is now considered evidence of the reality of systemic racial oppression, this minor flap became international news and the subject of hundreds of pages of opinionating. Amy Cooper was fired from her job and shamed, and her dog was (briefly) taken away. Public advocate Jumaane Williams held a press conference where he cried, called for Amy Cooper's immediate arrest, and indicated that had Christian Cooper not filmed the encounter, he would likely be in prison, if not dead.

The idea that Amy Cooper literally put Christian Cooper's life in danger because she called the police on him became an accepted part of the narrative. Eliza Orlins is a public defender who appeared on both *Survivor* and *The Amazing*

Race and is running to become Manhattan district attorney. In a *Washington Post* op-ed, Orlins fretted that "a spurious accusation in a park could mean a death sentence." Shawn T. Wooden, the black state treasurer of Connecticut, wondered, "If you're a black man, is curiosity a death sentence?"

Christian Cooper, too, mused over his brush with death. In an interview on MSNBC, he called the episode "sinister, potentially with more deadly consequences. I don't like to speculate as to whether or not that was—more deadly consequences were going to happen." The assumption that the NYPD would have responded to a midday dispute about dogs and birds in Central Park with guns blazing—as though they don't handle such matters every day as part of their jobs—is silly.

In fact, on a national level, the police commit very little violence, especially when you consider the fact that America has a fairly high rate of violent crime. Every year there are an estimated 375 million contacts between police and civilians. On average, about 1,000 of these interactions result in the police killing someone, almost invariably an armed or otherwise dangerous individual. In 2019, for instance, police killed 1,004 people, about 23 percent of whom were black. In total, according to the *Washington Post*, the police killed 9 unarmed blacks and 19 unarmed whites in the whole year. Given these data, it's hard to draw the conclusion that the country is irredeemably racist or that the police are wantonly violent—which is probably the reason why Black Lives Matter and associated groups rarely cite statistics, preferring to focus on the names and faces ("Say their names!") of specific victims.

In any case, the logic of the theory of institutional racism as it relates to criminal justice points unavoidably to ending enforcement of the law and abolishing the police. The argument is ineluctable: if involving the police to report a crime could implicate a black man, and the chance of his death at the hands of the police is unacceptably high, then we must abolish laws until we repair racism. We see this in the language of the supporters of the 2016 Criminal Justice Reform Act (CJRA), which was admittedly small potatoes compared to where the debate wound up just a few years later. And even though each supporter carefully pooh-poohed the idea that reducing penalties for littering, peeing in public, or smoking pot would mean decriminalization of those activities, that is effectively what has happened since then—as a walk through any Manhattan park or street will tell you soon enough.

Rory Lancman, a Queens council member and a strong supporter of the bill, made the cascade-effect argument when he described the

> extraordinary burden for those people who are charged with those offenses. Unlike if you fail to pay a parking ticket or fail to pay a Sanitation ticket. If you show—don't show up at a Summons Court hearing, a warrant will be issued for your arrest, and then the next time you have an interaction with a police officer of any kind, boy, you really will be in the Criminal Justice System.

Advocates always like to suggest that the law is softer on (rich) people who flout parking restrictions than on (poor) people who commit their own minor offenses. But if you don't pay your parking tickets, your car will be towed, and you will have to pay very steep penalties and fees to get it back. Furthermore, New York State will suspend your driver's license if you accrue enough unpaid tickets, and it is almost impossible to have parking tickets forgiven, whereas judges toss out citations all the time. It's hardly the case that drivers—most of whom aren't rich or white anyway—are considered above the law.

In his comments while voting for the CJRA, Donovan Richards, now the Queens borough president, somberly assured the city council that they "are righting a wrong, a systematic wrong that has taken place for far too long." According to Richards, "these summonses, these low-level offenses have stymied progress for so many young black and Latino communities across the city, and let's be clear: other communities share the same quality of life issues, but we are overly targeted."

The assertion that all races and neighborhoods share the "same quality of life issues" but that the police specifically target black and Latinos for enforcement is a received idea that gets little scrutiny. The issue comes up again and again, and the same arguments are always put forth. For example, in 2018 the council held an oversight hearing on disparate impact in marijuana enforcement. The legislators expressed dismay that 86 percent of the people arrested for marijuana offenses in 2016 were black or Latino, though blacks and Latinos are only 51.4 percent of the city's population.

Richards, then chair of the Public Safety Committee, described this difference as a "huge disparity." Rory

Lancman—who quit the city council to take a job in the governor's office—inveighed against the "grotesque disparities that exist between marijuana enforcement of people of color and white people." Andy Cohen from the Bronx—now a judge—said marijuana enforcement in New York City is "discriminatory in intent and certainly in effect."

And it's true: there is an evident disparity between the racial demographics of New York City and the population arrested for smoking marijuana in public. But similar disparities can be found across the spectrum of criminality, including crimes that are not subject to individual police discretion. For instance, in 2016, 84.7 percent of rape suspects, as reported by the victims, were black or Latino—almost the same percentage of people arrested for marijuana-related misdemeanors. Misdemeanor assault suspects, felony assault suspects, and murder suspects fall out along similar racial lines. Robbery suspects were 93.4 percent black and Latino, and shooting suspects were 97.6 percent black and Latino.

If relatively few robbers and violent criminals were black or Latino, it would be reasonable to look at the marijuana numbers and suggest that something is amiss. But given that all crimes are disproportionately committed by black and Latino New Yorkers, the assumption that arrests for smoking marijuana are driven by racial animus seems perverse, or least tendentious.

The fact is that arrests for "burning" marijuana are driven by community complaints. This can be demonstrated by observing that the neighborhoods with the most marijuana arrests are also where most serious crime takes place: 7 of the top 15 precincts for misdemeanor marijuana arrests are also among the most dangerous precincts by rate of major crime. This doesn't mean that open marijuana use leads directly to murder, felony assault, or grand larceny, but it's reasonable to conclude that smoking marijuana in public is more likely to be seen in high-crime neighborhoods than in lower-crime areas.

Indeed, open pot smoking is often closely connected with other forms of antisocial behavior, such as loitering in apartment lobbies, gambling, drinking alcohol, and fighting. Calls to the city's complaint line may result in the NYPD responding to a report that people are playing loud music on a front stoop; when the cops get there, it's not unusual to find a lit joint being passed around. The police may arrest someone for smoking marijuana, even though that wasn't really the main reason they were called. But that's not the same thing as saying that the police routinely patrol minority neighborhoods to round up black and Latino youth. Cops follow complaints.

· · · · · · · · · ·

The demonization of the police in New York City and the criminalization of normal police behavior accelerated under Mayor de Blasio. Social media and cell phones have certainly amplified the tendency. Arresting a resisting subject is never pretty: it can involve multiple officers pulling someone to the ground, manipulation of limbs and joints in directions counter to natural movement, "compliance strikes," and the use of batons or pepper sprays and even tasers or dogs. Such images can provoke reactions of disgust and rage and a sense that the police are essentially armed bullies, or just another gang of thugs.

Brutality does happen, of course—though the introduction of body cams demonstrates it much less than was anticipated by anti-cop activists and the plaintiffs' bar—and deserves condemnation when it's real. But the cause of public safety and trusted law enforcement is not served when elected officials jump on every WorldStarHipHop video and join the chorus of denunciation without getting all the facts or even caring to find out what they really are.

On December 7, 2018, a Brooklyn woman named Jazmine Headley went to the Human Resources Administration social services office to find out why she had stopped receiving vouchers for childcare for her one-year-old son. After waiting for three hours, unable to find a seat, she sat on the floor. As in most buildings open to the public and subject to fire and building codes, sitting on the floor was not allowed. Security officers—not NYPD officers, but NYC Human Resources Police Department "special officers"— asked Headley to get up. She quarreled with the officer and refused. She was told to leave the building and refused again.

Pretty soon, the scene devolved into a grotesquerie. The HRA officers called the NYPD. Cell phone video shows Jazmine Headley lying face down on the floor clutching her baby, who is screaming. As many as five uniformed officers from various offices stood over her, plucking at her while dozens of clients waiting for social services—none of whom, apparently, bothered to offer Headley their seat—surround them shrieking. Eventually, some of the cops grab the baby, and others try to manhandle Jazmine Headley in position to be handcuffed. Headley shouts, "My baby! You're hurting my baby!" In the ensuing fray, one of the officers was bitten and another was kicked hard enough to leave a big bruise. Headley wound up spending several days in jail.

In an ideal world, none of this would have happened. Ideally, no one would lose her voucher for an unexplained reason. The welfare office would have plenty of extra seats. Jazmine Headley would have been less obstreperous. The officers would have been a little more tolerant. The crowd of people bored silly sitting in a waiting room wouldn't have hyped up the confrontation into a hysterical frenzy. And politicians wouldn't have used this incident as an excuse to insert themselves in front of cameras and posture to demonstrate their righteous fury at the brutality of low-paid HRA peace officers.

But that's not the world we live in. The video of Jazmine Headley's arrest went viral, and the outrage machine started to whirr. The tableau of a poor, black single mother having her child ripped from her arms by armed police in a welfare office is overripe with significance for people invested in the narrative of the "criminalization of poverty," as City Council Majority Leader Laurie Cumbo put it. Cumbo decried the "clear racism" of the incident, which "puts a permanent stain on the police department. . . . [T]hose officers being fired is the least of what should happen here."

Regarding the charge of racism, it is probably worth noting that Jazmine Headley is a black woman—as were all the NYPD and HRA police and peace officers trying to arrest her. In fact, based on the available video, virtually everyone in the social services office—guards, clients, staff—was black. But being black, apparently, does not inoculate one from the demon of white supremacy. As Cumbo explained, the underlying racism of the officers led them to make a

> calculated decision that attacking this woman with her child was going to yield no repercussions. . . . [T]hat's why it's important to send a message that black women count, and when you attack black women . . . there will be repercussions.

Two months after the incident, which eventually resulted in the firing or resignation of 22 security guards, the city council held an oversight hearing to investigate the event. It was an orgy of tears and apologies. Corey Johnson, speaker of the city council, expressed deep contrition.

> I also want to apologize, I want to say I'm sorry, I'm sorry on behalf of the city of New York, I'm sorry you ever had to go to that HRA Center, I'm sorry that you and your baby had to experience that trauma, I'm sorry that you were wrongfully kept on Rikers Island for multiple days away from your family, you deserve so much more than you received and I am deeply, deeply apologetic that you had to have this experience.

Laurie Cumbo, taking a second and third bite at the apple, read aloud from Sojourner Truth's speech, "Ain't I a Woman." She then wept and invited Headley to visit the Sesame Place theme park with her and her own son. "Thank you," the councilwoman said.

Helen Rosenthal, a councilmember from the Upper West Side of Manhattan, observed that all the HRA workers, not just the security guards, deserved blame.

> The first failure is with the HRA workers. . . . [T]he minute someone saw her on the floor someone should have sat down next to her and said, "Wow. This must be a really rotten situation for you. This is awful. How are you?" And how that could not be the first response of an employee is beyond me.

Rosenthal also demanded to know why "survivor-centric and trauma-based" policing was not offered when the officers showed up to find Jazmine Headley refusing to get off the floor.

Mayor de Blasio chimed in, too, with predictably fulsome concern. "I want to just say as a parent, my heart goes out Ms. Headley and to her son," he commiserated. "I can't imagine what it must feel like to have that happen. It's just deeply, deeply troubling and no mother should go through that and no child should go through it."

He also made a gesture of magnanimity, restoring Headley's child-care voucher by decree. "Whatever benefits are due to her, we'll make sure they're granted immediately," Mayor de Blasio announced loftily, bestowing his largesse like a wise king in a fairy tale. A year later, the city settled a lawsuit brought by Jazmine Headley; to compensate her for her troubles, she was awarded $625,000.

But amidst all this apologizing, second-guessing, and hastening to make amends, no one asked if it is actually okay just to sit on the floor of a government office and refuse to get up. There was no medical emergency that caused Headley to sit on the ground; she wasn't in distress or feeble. Helen Rosenthal's insistence that HRA clerks ought to have rushed to Headley's aid and put their arm around her smacks of the highest degree of condescension, both to Headley and to the hypothetical worker. This wasn't a refugee camp for the recently cluster-bombed—it was a municipal welfare office where dealing with bored, footsore, and querulous clients all day long is standard fare and where the people seeking public assistance have a pretty good idea of what to expect.

And as with the Eric Garner case, nobody looks at it from the point of view of a security officer whose job—whose sworn duty, in fact—is to maintain order. There are reasons why public buildings post "maximum occupancy" signs, have multiple points of egress and clearly lighted exit signs and in the event of an emergency, the halls have to be clear. Should sitting on the floor be allowed, and if so, how about lying on the floor? The officials and members of the press who are horrified that the clerks and guards weren't more sympathetic to Headley betray their own disdain for her. They think it is absurd to expect people waiting in a government office for public assistance to have patience or behave in a civilized manner because they have nothing but contempt for the poor, whom they secretly deplore. Their underlying attitude is no different from a snob who would watch a video of the Headley episode and smirk, "Well, what would you expect?"

This becomes obvious when you look at the even lower regard in which the security guards were held. HRA police, while technically peace officers, are low status. Their job has no glamour, no respect, and low pay; it is staffed largely by black women—much like the population they are supposed to be monitoring. Their job is thankless, and no thanks is exactly what they got when they told Jazmine Headley to get up and she told them to leave her alone.

New York City's elite, from Mayor de Blasio on down, demand safe streets and safe spaces for the people of New York. But by refusing to stand up for law enforcement officers when they try to do their jobs, our public officials impart an inconsistent message to law enforcement, who develop a version of learned helplessness. Not knowing which uses of force are going to wind up in a viral video, get them fired, or make them the object of a scolding lecture from a posturing city council member has a demoralizing effect and induces a hesitancy to engage with the public, even when action is called for. This makes New York less safe.

· · · · · · · · · ·

One of the prime movers of the decriminalization drive in New York has been Jumaane Williams, formerly a city councilman and then "public advocate"—a citywide elected position with little authority but plenty of ceremony—who functions as a kind of glorified ombudsman. It's a highly paid role that comes with a 24-hour NYPD security detail, a chauffeured SUV, and zero responsibilities. If a public advocate wanted to go on vacation for his or her whole four-year term, it's unlikely that anyone would miss him or her.

Williams, a supporter of Black Lives Matter, has gained national prominence for his role as an "elected activist," as he describes himself. Reared in the Flatbush neighbor-hood of Brooklyn, which he also represented in the council, Williams had a spotty career as the owner of a vegan café and "housing organizer" before winning election in 2009. He was one of a group of insurgents, backed by the Working Families Party (WFP), who came to power that year, defeat-ing centrist Democrats in the primary. They formed a self-styled "Progressive Caucus" in the council and were close allies with de Blasio, who assumed the public advocate's role in that same election.

Jumaane Williams likes to call attention to what he sees as hypocrisies regarding policing and public order. These frequently veer into the absurd. In 2014, debating stop-and-frisk on CNN, Williams made the point that "we don't want to live in a police state. And if we want to violate [civil rights], . . . we can't just do it in the black and brown com-munity." He went on to note that police "don't do it on Wall Street. We don't stop and frisk people with briefcases. . . ." When another guest observed that there aren't shootings on Wall Street, Jumaane Williams retorted, "Yes, but there's financial crimes that cause the shootings."

These broken logical chains of cause and effect are typi-cal of high-level policy debate in New York City, where non sequiturs such as, "let's fight gun crime by frisking bank-ers, who don't carry guns, but shootings are their fault any-way"—which would not pass muster in a junior high school debate club—are received as Solomonic pronouncements. I cannot overemphasize this point: elected officials in New York City frequently speak absolute nonsense, but for reasons I will explain in my conclusion, nobody calls them on their double-talk.

In 2012, Williams sponsored a resolution calling on the city "to stop arresting people for committing minor infractions in the transit system, irrespective of whether they have an arrest record or have previously committed minor infractions in the system." These "minor infractions" included "littering, sleeping, occupying more than one seat, and placing a foot on a seat." The resolution noted that "in addition to being very disruptive, an arrest can cause significant stress, financial hardship, loss of employment and difficulty in finding employment, among other things."

It may sound unduly harsh to be arrested for sleeping on the subway or taking up two seats, but in fact very few people are or were actually arrested for these violations. The resolution—which did not pass—gives away the real purpose of the law when it explains that it applies "irrespective of whether they have an arrest record or have previously committed minor infractions in the system." The point of making it possible for the police to arrest someone for what seems like a picayune trespass is to give them a range of tools to address disorderly behavior. The cops don't go around arresting people who drop a scrap of paper on the trains or who nod off on their way home from work, but a habitual subway sleeper taking up an entire bench of seats might not respond to a nudge or even to a citation. Sometimes an arrest is the only way to get a miscreant off the car.

Williams's resolution calling for an end to arrests on the subway was not passed by the council. It was largely ignored.

But its 2012 introduction demonstrates how radical ideas percolate through the culture, both up and down. By 2019, there were calls of increasing volume to "depolice" the subway. In October of that year, cops were filmed on a Brooklyn subway platform breaking up a scrum of youths having a battle royale well after midnight. One belligerent youth claimed he was abused by an officer and filed an intention to sue the city. In a separate incident, also caught on camera, police arrested a turnstile jumper who was believed to be carrying a gun. These episodes were widely condemned as militarization of the transit system. Williams demanded NYPD disinvestment, condemning the "excessive use of force and hyperaggressive policing we saw in these two incidents."

On the last day of January 2020 a movement called "J31," which demanded no law enforcement on the subway and free transit for everyone, staged a major set of actions throughout the transit system. Protesters chanted "Fuck the Police," decried the racism of the police department, and sabotaged fare collection systems. They carried a large banner reading, "Ante Up! Punch that Cop!! NYPD out of MTA!" In a prelude to the larger-scale riots to come later that year, garbage cans were set ablaze in the subway system, and protesters pointed lasers at cops' eyes.

Meanwhile, as crime continued to spread throughout New York City, Jumaane Williams—who has labored more intensively than any other official to hamper police effectiveness—blamed the police for failing to act to contain violence. In a letter to police commissioner Dermot Shea, Williams took the NYPD to task for dragging its feet amid "a horrific rise in shootings . . . with the vast majority of victims being black and brown New Yorkers." Williams upbraided the NYPD, reminding Commissioner Shea that "community trust" in the police can "degrade from underenforcement." This is a typical maneuver by critics like Williams, who leaves himself room to denounce the police whether they do or don't do their jobs to his satisfaction.

Williams has a long history of tangling with the police. At the West Indian Day Parade in 2011, he intentionally crossed into a "frozen zone" meant to control a crowd of more than a million people. He claims that he identified himself as an elected official and was arrested anyway; he later insisted that the arrest was racially motivated.

In 2012, he attended a one-year anniversary commemoration of the end of the "occupation" of Zuccotti Park to "observe and ensure the rights of protestors are being protected." Police attempted to establish a secure perimeter; video shows Williams ignoring their requests not to stand on a bench. An officer pushed him away, but he continued to crowd the police line. In 2018, protesting the attempted deportation of convicted mortgage fraudster Ravi Ragbir, Jumaane Williams was arrested while blocking Broadway. He scrapped with the police and then sat in front of an ambulance.

In 2020, following weeks of agitation to defund the police department, Williams claimed that he would use his "charter-mandated" powers to paralyze the city if police funding was not cut to his satisfaction. He said that a clause in the city charter requires the public advocate's approval before property tax warrants can be distributed. Thus, he claimed, it lay within his authority to freeze the city's ability to collect revenue necessary for running its operations. Mayor de Blasio, to his credit, dismissed this idea as absurd, and nothing came of it.

Williams has promoted radical expansion of funding for "violence interrupters" as a means of "curing violence," despites the tactic's dubious efficacy. He has demanded "abolition" of jails. He regularly calls any disparity in law enforcement racist, though there is evident racial disparity in criminal activity. He insists, and has for years, that social workers should answer calls for emotionally disturbed persons instead of police officers.

But it's easy to want less policing when you live in the city's safest and best-guarded gated community. Almost as soon as he was elected to citywide office—and no longer required to live in his central Brooklyn home district—Williams moved within the confines of the Fort Hamilton Army Base. Fort Hamilton, New York's only active military garrison, sits boldly at the southwest corner of Brooklyn at the foot of the Verrazano-Narrows Bridge, guarding the entrance to New York Harbor. Its residences, which are mostly meant to house military families, are open to "qualified members" of the general public.

Fort Hamilton is fenced in by a secure perimeter guarded 24/7 by military police, which man its two entrances. Access to the base is tightly controlled; "all visitors and uncleared contractors desiring access to Fort Hamilton must be vetted" through national crime databases, per the fort's website. Williams, in other words, is safe as can be.

As the holder of a citywide office, he can live anywhere he wants. As soon as he could, he deserted his home district of Flatbush and moved to a federally guarded military installation, where you need REAL ID–compliant documentation to enter. He is whisked in and out, in a chauffeured SUV, by his round-the-clock, city-funded NYPD security squad.

There are no drive-by shootings at Fort Hamilton. There are no homeless people. No open-air shooting galleries. No menacing druggies. Protesters frequently hold actions outside the homes of officials they wish to harass into supporting their radical agenda; for instance, Black Lives Matter, a group Williams supports, went to Police Benevolent Association President Pat Lynch's house to scream "All Cops Are Bastards" and other imprecations. Members of the Democratic Socialists of America, demanding total defunding of the NYPD, hammered on the front doors of city councilmembers in opposition. Williams is blissfully immune from such scary insults; even if someone wanted to protest him at home peacefully, heor she would be unable to do so, because he or she would have to breach a US Army barricade.

Jumaane Williams represents the ultimate hypocrisy of the elected radical class. He has a fevered vision of a just society that he promotes tirelessly. But when it comes time to harvest and eat the stunted fruit of his labor, he deserts the field and leaves the gleanings for his suffering constituents.

· · · · · · · · · ·

Kalief Browder was a 22-year-old Bronx man who committed suicide by hanging himself in his parents' home in 2015. He had spent three years in jail on Rikers Island, much of it in solitary confinement, and was never convicted of the crime for which he had been arrested shortly before his seventeenth birthday. Wracked with depression and anxiety, Browder tried to kill himself several times before finally succeeding, two years after finally being released.

The details of the story, originally reported in a blockbuster 2014 *New Yorker* article and then in a major television documentary produced by Jay-Z, are heartbreaking to consider. They have been repeated many times: accused of nothing more than stealing a backpack, Kalief Browder was remanded to jail because his family was too poor to afford bail. He was consigned to rot in solitary confinement and all but forgotten. This story became a *cause célèbre* and has arguably had a more consequential impact on trends in criminal justice reform—both in New York and nationally—than any other event in recent American history.

In 2016, when President Obama announced an end to solitary confinement for juveniles in federal detention and limits on its use for other offenders, he highlighted the case of Kalief Browder as an illustration of its failure. When the New York State legislature eliminated cash bail as a condition of pretrial release for almost all but the most serious felonies and all misdemeanors, Senate Majority Leader Andrea Stewart-Cousins announced that New York would "make sure that we're not criminalizing poverty, and that there would never, ever, ever be another instance of a Kalief Browder." And the movement to close the city's jail complex on Rikers Island was specifically organized around the memory of Kalief Browder, who was cited at the city council vote as the prevailing spirit of the crusade.

It's curious that so many details of the Kalief Browder story, as reported in the original *New Yorker* article, have been overlooked or ignored in the rush to construct a compelling narrative. Browder was not arrested simply for "stealing a backpack," as Stewart-Cousins repeated. In fact, he was accused of chasing and beating up a Mexican immigrant named Roberto Bautista and stealing his backpack, which was filled with electronic equipment and $700 in cash.

It's also not true that because "he didn't have the resources to get out of jail, that he would languish there for three years," in the words of Senator Stewart-Cousins. Kalief Browder originally had bail set at $3,000, a sum his mother was able to meet. But the bail was rejected when it emerged that Browder was already on probation for having stolen and crashed a bakery truck several months before. According to New York State law at the time, people on probation were generally ineligible for bail. And while it is true that Browder spent a long period of time in solitary confinement, it is also the case that he was sent there for constant fighting, including an attack on a guard.

There's no question—none—that Kalief Browder's situation was grotesque and that he was ill served by the system. Regardless of his criminal record or the seriousness of the charge, or even if he was violent in jail, there was no reason for him to sit in Rikers for three years, much of it in punitive segregation, awaiting trial. But the feature of his story that most starkly cries out for reform—though it hasn't received it—is the government's delay in delivering speedy justice in resolving his case. Indeed, he or his attorney appeared before a judge dozens of times, with the prosecution asking for repeated adjournments, even though they were supposed to be ready.

Browder was, in truth, offered deals that would have sprung him immediately in exchange for an admission of guilt, but he insisted on going to trial to prove his innocence—certainly his right under our system of jurisprudence, but a naive expectation regarding the notorious Bronx County Court, which is a dysfunctional mess.

It is noteworthy—though seldom noted—that one of the judges who oversaw Browder's case, and before whom he appeared on multiple occasions, was none other than current Bronx District Attorney Darcel Clark. It's a testament to the power of the New York City political establishment to see no evil on the part of its members, even when one of them was responsible for the persecution of one of the clique's primary martyrs. Clark even promoted the assistant district attorney who led the bungled prosecution of Kalief Browder.

In any event, the Browder case was made to fit a convenient narrative in the service of criminal justice reform. But the resulting reforms of the bail system and pretrial detention at Rikers Island were based on misstatements of fact and the repetition of cherished myths about who goes to jail and why. Following the enactment of bail reform, the crime rate in New York City spiked, and it continues to rise, as even dangerous criminals are promptly returned to the streets.

To listen to advocates of bail reform, decriminalization, and decarceration, our prisons and jails are filled with non-violent individuals, largely imprisoned for minor crimes like marijuana possession. In September 2018, Robert F. Kennedy

Human Rights, a charitable organization, announced a plan to pay the bail of every woman and minor held in New York City's jails. According to the group, run by Kerry Kennedy, the slain senator's daughter, "access to justice depends on whether you can afford bail. The majority of people incarcerated in the notoriously violent Rikers Island are behind bars for the crime of being too poor."

This is a favorite theme of criminal justice reformers, but most Rikers inmates are accused of serious crimes. Typically, around 11 percent of the population is there for murder, attempted murder, or manslaughter; 20 percent are in for robbery or burglary; and another 25 percent face charges involving weapons, felony assault, sale of drugs, or rape or other sexual offenses. New York's jails are not crowded with people whose only crime was jumping a subway turnstile or smoking weed; the average number of people held in Rikers on a given day in 2019 for fare beating was two, and for pot possession, one.

It is also commonly said that pretrial detention contingent on bail is inherently unjust because people being held for trial have not been found guilty of a crime. Speaking in support of "Kalief's Law," a bill that would improve criminal justice proceedings in order to guarantee speedy trials, Assemblyman Jeffrion Aubry commented, "Every moment we sit in silence, every moment we surrender to complacency, thousands of Kalief Browders are being churned through this broken system—thousands of inmates continue to sit in jail without Due Process."

But while it is true that people in jail awaiting trial for a crime they have allegedly committed are technically innocent, it is not the case that they are being held without due process. In order to remand someone to jail or assign bail, a judge typically has determined that there is probable cause that the suspect will be found guilty of the crime. While this finding is tentative, and certainly unpleasant to the actually innocent, it is part of the due process of law.

After heated criticism from the NYPD, Robert F. Kennedy Human Rights terminated its "Mass Bail Out" program to "end wealth-based detention." The group did its cause no favors by bailing out 18-year-old Rickeem Parker one week after the eight-time arrestee was captured on video brutally beating a corrections officer. Parker then skipped bail, not showing up for his next court date.

But following the passage of bail reform, which went into effect on the first day of 2020, the work of Robert F. Kennedy Human Rights was made more or less obsolete anyway. New York State completely reconfigured its system of pretrial detention. People arrested for all misdemeanors—including violent crimes like assault—and all nonviolent felonies could no longer be required to post bail as a condition of their release. Domestic abuse and weapons charges were ostensibly exempted, though cases quickly emerged of heinous offenders being returned to the streets immediately. New York State is almost unique in not allowing judges to consider community safety as a reason to impose bail or hold an arrestee in remand—ensuring his or her return to court is the only permissible consideration.

One of the advantages of forcing criminals to cough up bail is that it allows them to cool their heels in jail for a day or so. The well-documented stultifying boredom of a holding cell is often enough to drain the urgency out of a street squabble and give the parties a chance to reflect on the deeper meaning of their life choices. The "incapacitation effect," or the fact that people in jail are simply unable to commit crimes against the public, is not insubstantial, either.

When we look at the statistics of who was actually held in jail on bail, we see that very few people were there for trivial amounts. Most people assigned bail of less than $500 were able to scrounge it together, and many whose families were "unable to raise bail" remained in jail because their loved ones were tired of dealing with them. Three out of four Rikers' pretrial detainees have been there before, and their average age is over 35. The families of hardened, career criminals are often the ones who are first victimized by their reprobate relations, and it's on the sofas of grandmothers, aunts, siblings, and girlfriends that bailed-out cons wind up flopping. Sometimes these poor souls have had enough and decide that tough love, in the form of not paying their relative's bail, is the last resort.

But even before bail reform passed in Albany, Mayor de Blasio and the local district attorneys had begun releasing younger defendants in advance of trial and putting an increasing number of arrestees into "diversion" programs, even for serious crimes. For example, New York City is notoriously tough on illegal gun possession. It is very hard to obtain a permit even to own a handgun just to keep at home, much less to be allowed to carry one on one's person. Being caught with an illegal gun in New York City is supposed to carry a stiff, mandatory 40-month prison sentence, though the law includes loopholes that give judges and prosecutors substantial latitude to impose lesser sentences "in the interest of justice."

Brooklyn District Attorney Eric Gonzalez has been extraordinarily lenient in his prosecution of gun crimes. In 2019, his office diverted 30 percent of gun possession guilty pleas to youth diversion programs, where offenders have their records sealed after completing an 18-month educational course. Several of the diverted youth were quickly rearrested on new weapons charges after they were caught toting guns. But despite an increase of shootings in Brooklyn North throughout 2019, Gonzalez persevered in his efforts to reduce incarceration by, as he put it in his "Justice 2020 Initiative" action plan, "making jail the 'alternative.'" Even before the state reformed its bail laws, Gonzalez boasted that he had reduced by 58 percent the number of people being held on bail in misdemeanor cases. He also promised to pursue early release for convicted felons as soon as "the minimum sentence is complete."

Justice 2020 promotes the premise that New York relies on "overincarceration" to handle its crime problem—which at base should be dealt with as a systemic problem requiring more services and interventions. But the whole idea of mass incarceration—that our prisons and jails are filled with nonviolent first offenders—is simply incorrect. Less than 10 percent of people arrested in New York City even wind up with a jail admission, and less than 2 percent of all arrests result in a prison sentence.

Of the people actually serving a prison sentence in New York State, 64 percent of them have been convicted of a violent felony. Of these violent felons, 20 percent are murderers, and the rest are rapists, people convicted of assault or first-degree manslaughter, kidnappers, people who held up stores with guns, and so on. Among the 36 percent of inmates who are not categorized specifically as "violent felons," the state includes people convicted of second-degree manslaughter, "other homicide," and "other sex offenses." About 12 percent of the incarcerated population was convicted of a drug charge.

These numbers are reflected nationally. The myth of American prisons as filled with nonviolent drug offenders—the fabled black kid with a joint who winds up doing 10 years of hard time—is simply false. Some proponents of the anti-incarceration movement are honest enough to admit that shutting down the prison system means letting killers and rapists out on the streets. They balance the risk to public safety against what they see as the inhumane brutality of the prison system and accept the tradeoff. Except most of them—living in pleasant suburbs, well-policed urban neighborhoods, peaceful college towns, or like Jumaane Williams, on fortified army bases—will never have to swallow a dose of their own evil medicine.

· · · · · · · · · ·

No sensible person claims that Rikers Island has no problems. Most of New York City's jails sit on the island, located between Queens and the Bronx, that was mostly constructed out of landfill. It's home to 10 jails, including a facility for women, a jail for youthful offenders, and several men's jails of varying levels of security. The island is huge, fairly self-contained, and accessible only by a bridge that connects it to Queens.

Rikers is unusual among American jails in that it holds prisoners from five different jurisdictions—the boroughs of New York City—each of which is a county with its own prosecutor and courthouse. Thus criminals awaiting trial in the Bronx or Staten Island may be jailed on Rikers Island and have to be bused across the city to attend hearings or trials. In most places, the county jail is connected to or at least near the courthouse. The process of busing and escorting hundreds of inmates to courtrooms around the city is laborious and expensive. The isolation of the jail from the courts also makes it hard for lawyers to see their clients and arguably can negatively impact trial preparation. Getting to Rikers is an enormously time-consuming process, so families and friends must spend a whole day getting to the island, usually by public transportation, going through security at a visitors' processing center and then taking a shuttle bus to the specific jail where their loved one is held.

Part of the problem with Rikers is that the jails are old and falling apart; an inspection concluded that inmates are easily able to use rusting and rotting parts of the infrastructure to make weapons. Many of the jails were designed and built more than 50 years ago, when prison construction standards still dictated that cells ought to be built in blocks stacked atop one another, with correction officers circulating but not in direct view of the inmates most of the time. The prisoners have to be removed from the block to eat and for recreation. Starting in the 1980s, a new model of prison design based on direct supervision came into vogue, whereby cells are organized as pods that include their eating space and are adjacent to their yard for outdoor time. Rikers, built in the old mode, contains poor lines of sight, which make it harder to keep inmates from fighting, dealing in contraband, or preparing to attack guards.

The push to close Rikers was driven by the same narrative force that drove bail reform and other contemporary criminal justice reform measures: the idea that, as Councilman Donovan Richards stated, echoing Michelle Alexander's now-seminal though seriously flawed work, that "mass incarceration" represents "the new Jim Crow," and inmates on Rikers are "living in a hellhole." Formulated by a blue-ribbon commission led by Jonathan Lippman, a former chief judge of the New York State Court of Appeals, the report, entitled, "A More Just New York City," specifically cited the case of Kalief Browder, which noted that "the problems of the criminal justice system, particularly around the issue of race, were crystallized" by his suicide. "Browder's story," the report continues, "remains a powerful rallying cry for those interested in forging a more just and humane justice system."

Rikers is legendarily brutal, and the push to close it down entirely has been driven in large part by the horrific tales of violence that have emerged from its depths. "A big part of the problem," the Lippman Report concludes, "is the model that Rikers Island embodies. The sheer size of the inmate population creates management challenges." But counterintuitively, even as the incarcerated population in the city's jails has fallen, violence has gotten much worse. The average daily population in 1998 was about 17,500, and inmates committed about 6,500 violent crimes. In 2018, the number of prisoners had dropped to around 9,500, yet the number of violent assaults had almost doubled, to almost 13,000.

Part of the reason that violence soared on Rikers Island, even while the number of prisoners fell to historic lows, certainly owes to measures that Mayor de Blasio took to limit the range of disciplinary options that corrections officers are permitted to use to punish violent inmates. In the first three years of his mayoralty, the de Blasio administration gradually forbid the use of "punitive segregation" for inmates under the age of 22, even though youthful offenders commit the majority of jail violence.

The Lippman Report set forth a plan to close Rikers entirely, replacing it with smaller, more humane, borough-based "community jails." The original plan spoke of reducing the average daily number of inmates from about 10,000 in 2017 to roughly 5,000 in 2026, when the new jails were to be completed. But when local communities objected to the proposed size of the new jails—the Manhattan jail was to be 45 stories high, and the one in Brooklyn would have 39 floors—the target number of inmates was suddenly cut to 3,300.

This one-third drop from the earlier 5,000 estimate was not driven by a decrease in crime—indeed, some serious crimes were trending up—but by the demands of council members in whose districts the new jails would be sited and who refused to approve the construction of larger jails. The city thus allowed political considerations to dictate how large its new jails can be and then tailored prisoner population estimates to fit those circumstances. The new estimate confirmed suspicions that the entire project of closing Rikers was never really about the poor conditions of the city's existing jails at all. In fact, the brutality of life on Rikers, as "crystallized" in the case of Kalief Browder, was the bait in order to ram through a radical transformation of the entire system of criminal justice in New York City.

The city planned to cut the number of people in jail through decriminalization of QoL offenses and the elimination of cash bail—but a target of 3,300 inmates represents an aggressively optimistic view of the future of crime in New York City and would require a significant realignment of expectations about public safety. The number of people in jail in New York City is historically low, due to concerted efforts to divert low-level offenders into incarceration alternatives. The remaining incarcerated population largely represents a core group of hardened, violent, habitual criminals. Council Speaker Corey Johnson attributed the reduction of the estimated population from 5,000 to 3,300 to bail reform. The remainder of the reduction, he explained, will represent people no longer sent back to jail, as they are now, after violating "technical" provisions of their parole, such as "missing curfew." In reality, few parolees get remanded to prison simply for minor violations of the rules, and when they do, they spend only limited time in Rikers before being sent back to prison upstate.

Simply speaking, reducing the number of people in jail below 3,300 demands fewer arrests and the immediate release of serious criminals following arraignment. It implies not just decarceration or alternative punishments to jail and prison but also de facto decriminalization or less enforcement of the law to limit the number of people who wind up behind bars. This agenda is not confined to the radical left—the anarchists who tried to burn down a Seattle police station and who occupied New York's City Hall Park, demanding the defunding of the NYPD. It is the stated goal of a major segment of the city's criminal justice complex and is backed by a sizable minority of its elected officials. The "No New Jails" coalition, which demands the closure of Rikers Island without replacing the lost capacity, has pushed its abolitionist argument into the mainstream.

For instance, the respected Legal Aid Society, which receives hundreds of millions in city and state dollars to provide legal services to indigent defendants, condemns the "false binary of the Close Rikers plan," which is "inextricably linked to the gentrification that has gutted Black and Latinx communities." The organization demands "a future with zero jails in our city, zero jails in our state, and zero jails in our country." Assembly member Yuh-Line Niou, who represents the district that will house the Manhattan jail, argues against the new plan on the basis that "our system criminalizes poverty through mandatory surcharges and fees which create modern day debtors' prisons." No evidence exists that anyone in New York City is incarcerated due to such fees.

Common sense tells us that smaller jails may mean fewer inmates—but not fewer criminals. By the beginning of 2020, the jailed population was already down to about 5,700; by March, bail reform and other measures had reduced the number of inmates to 5,450. But when the pandemic hit and New York City announced widespread quarantine measures, pressure grew to expedite the rapid release of prisoners to keep them safe from COVID-19 infection. Almost immediately the incarcerated population fell to levels unseen in New

York City since the 1940s. By mid-April there were fewer than 4,000 inmates on Rikers and in all the other city jails.

About 130 of the inmates released because of the pandemic were facing violent felony charges—a worrisome data point. Another 230 of the released inmates were classed as "nonviolent felony detainees." But just because the charge you're in jail for right now is not a violent felony, that doesn't make you a practitioner of nonviolence. As the writer on criminal justice Rafael Mangual has noted, "Felons aren't specialists." A rapist may steal a car; a burglar may beat someone up. Most criminals are opportunists, and their general orientation is to achieve their immediate goals through whatever means are available to them. It is false comfort to assume that a "nonviolent felony detainee" is someone you'd trust to babysit your kids.

As the Mayor's Office on Criminal Justice (MOCJ) statistics reported at the end of May 2020, "in the face of the current public health emergency, the number of New Yorkers held in NYC jails has plummeted, shrinking by 27% in ten weeks, a steeper population decline than in all of last year." Connecting the "plummeting" decline in the jail population, along with the elimination of bail for most offenses, to the sudden jump in violent crime seems obvious. But when NYPD Commissioner Dermot Shea suggested this link, critics pounced, noting that the number of arrested recidivists was small compared to the total number of people released under bail reform or for pandemic-related reasons. But with some 80 percent of shootings going unsolved, there's no telling how many of them were really committed by released criminals.

The data that are available regarding pretrial release don't promise amazing results. In 2019, before bail reform and COVID-19, about 5,650 people were on "supervised release," a 20 percent increase from 2018. MOCJ boasts, "citywide, 87% of Supervised Release participants attend every court appearance and 90% are not rearrested for a felony while they are in the program," which means that 10 percent are rearrested for a felony. That's 565 people who were arrested for a serious crime, let out on conditional release, and then committed another serious crime, for which they were caught. This doesn't include all the felonies committed by members of this cohort for which nobody has been arrested yet. One can only imagine that the thousands of additional people released from city jails and state prison are—based on statistical history—responsible for at least part of the recent sharp increase in crime.

4

Socialist Dreams:
Spending Every Dime

I N THE RUN-UP TO his campaign for the presidency, Bill de Blasio rehearsed a new slogan to shout on the hustings. "There's plenty of money in this town," he said, pausing in case the imaginary crowds of enthusiastic supporters wanted to complete the line in unison. "It's just in the wrong hands!" At this point he would wait for applause and cheers, which resounded only in his mind, alas.

Though de Blasio always cites President Franklin D. Roosevelt, Mayor Fiorello LaGuardia, and labor reformer Frances Perkins as his models, none of his New Deal heroes was ever quite so vulgar in the nakedness of their appeal to outright class warfare. Huey Long may be more appropriate, though, to be honest, populist demagogic drapery has never really hung correctly on de Blasio: ultimately a well-mannered Boston snob with multiple generations of Ivy League in his background, eating pizza with a knife and fork.

De Blasio's leftist economic philosophy owes more to his sentimental solidarity-movement 1980s sojourns in Central America, informed by the romance of peasant expropriation of *latifundia* and the subtle casuistries of liberation theology—the ideal religion for intellectual atheists, who can't stomach the ineffable unless it is rooted firmly in the dialectic. Let's not forget, after all, de Blasio's Miami campaign-trail gaffe, when—forgetting which Latinos he was talking to—he clumsily saluted striking airport workers with Che Guevara's signature exhortation, "*Hasta la victoria, siempre!*" ("Forever onward to victory!"). There went Florida.

Napoleon said, "To understand the man you have to know what was happening in the world when he was twenty." In 1981, when de Blasio turned 20, Ronald Reagan had just taken office, and the left was in a paroxysm of despair. As the herald of the rise of a new Christian fascism, Reagan embodied hate: hate for racial minorities, for the urban poor, for the third world, and for women. The liberal consciousness of the era crystalized around Reagan as the manifestation of intolerance, unreason, and vicious greed.

Reagan continues to occupy prominent space in de Blasio's mind. The election of Reagan, he told *The Atlantic* in 2015, "was a shock like you would not believe." He refers to the election of 1980 constantly as the moment when the New Deal/Great Society era of massive government spending on social engineering projects was betrayed, and the "millionaires and billionaires," as he always says, took control.

It's been all downhill since then. Hence his constant focus on inequality, and the theme of the "tale of two cities," where the rich fatten themselves from the sweat of the poor, who scrape for orts and slops.

De Blasio retails the politics of resentment and is refreshingly candid about it. This simplistic outlook—that the haves have stolen from the have-nots—colors all his policies and their justifications. To understand the Progressive approach to budgeting, spending, economic development, and labor relations, we must grasp the extent to which its perspective is rooted in a socialist worldview. He might call it "democratic socialism," but there is nothing democratic about this socialism—it is centrally managed and top-down all the way.

Consider his comment in December 2020 regarding the middle school admissions process. "I like to say very bluntly, our mission is to redistribute wealth," de Blasio explained. "A lot of people bristle at that phrase—that is in fact the phrase we need to use." Some people might ask how eliminating "screening" for entry to sixth grade connects to class struggle and the reallocation of riches, but if you are familiar with Progressive reasoning, you should understand that logic is beside the point, because every public policy is about wealth inequality and thus racial inequality and the eradication of white privilege. It's just a matter of capturing the subtle rhetoric that justifies the action.

The problem for Progressive commissars and social engineers in America's city halls is that it's hard for municipalities to do much about redistributing wealth on the grand scale that they would prefer. Cities have no constitutional authority in our republican system and are legally "creatures of the state." Mayors have limited powers to collect revenue and are easily checked by governors. Outside of Barcelona in 1937, there are few models of municipal socialism that dictators manqué like Bill de Blasio can look to.

But de Blasio was never shy about encouraging New Yorkers to resent and loathe their better-off neighbors. "You haven't been paid what you deserve for all the hard work. You haven't been given the time you deserve. You're not living the life you deserve. And here is the cold, hard truth—it's no accident," said the mayor in his 2019 "state of the city" address. According to de Blasio, the struggles of life are part of a sinister design—a conspiracy against the many. He continued

> It's an agenda. An agenda that's dominated our politics from Reaganomics to the Trump tax giveaway to the wealthy and corporations. For decades. For decades, working people have done their share. For decades, working people have gotten more and more productive. At the same time, they've gotten a smaller and smaller share of the wealth they create. Here's the truth. Brothers and sisters, there's plenty of money in the world. There's plenty of money in this city. It's just in the wrong hands.

All the major problems of society can be traced to Ronald Reagan, who, conveniently, is to blame for many of the problems of New York City—even such local, pedestrian matters as the boilers and leaky roofs of the city's public housing projects. Confronted about his consistent failure to provide basic services to the 400,000 New Yorkers living in the nation's largest public housing system—which is falling apart, and where 80 percent of the residents report losing heat or hot water during the winter—the mayor blames Reagan.

Speaking in January 2020, de Blasio claimed that the New York City Housing Authority (NYCHA) had

> now gone through about 40 years of systematic disin-vestment because of what's happened in Washington. . . . Where is the federal government we knew from the 1930s to 1980—actually, 1933, I should say, to 1980—that actually was a major partner in affordable housing?

Asking de Blasio about NYCHA is almost guaranteed to bring a mention of Reagan's election in 1980 as the moment when things began to go wrong. "I think we can say that the physical decline of NYCHA dates to 1980," de Blasio said in June 2018, "and this is not a partisan statement, this is an analytical statement. When Ronald Reagan was elected is when the federal government started pulling back from support for public housing."

In February 2019, the mayor explained that "the entire concept of public housing was that it was chartered by the federal government on the assumption of adequate fed-eral support and that started to change with the election of Ronald Reagan in 1980 and it got worse and worse and worse."

De Blasio subscribes to a version of history—for public housing and in general—that sees the New Deal as a moment of historic promise, steadily fulfilled through the era of postwar prosperity and amplified by the Great Society's expansion of the welfare state before climaxing under Jimmy Carter. Then the neoliberal reforms of the Reagan era began rolling back decades of progress. The broken elevators and leaky pipes in thousands of NYCHA buildings aren't just Ronald Reagan's fault, of course. The mayor also blames Newt Gingrich and the 1994 GOP Congress, along with Rudy Giuliani and Mike Bloomberg, the Republican mayors who preceded him. He blames Governor Cuomo and New York state, too, for failing to make up the $20 billion short-fall in NYCHA's capital budget.

We don't have to get deep in the weeds on NYCHA history, but the facts shine a light on how poorly the city manages a major asset—belying Progressive claims that socialized housing needs to be implemented vigorously and that other elements of urban life, such as the power grid, ought to be publicly owned—and also on certain sobering realities behind New York's budgetary crisis. But suffice to note that the mayor's narrative doesn't square with the facts.

NYCHA's operating revenue for the 2019 fiscal year totaled $3.5 billion; rent paid by tenants accounted for 30 percent of that amount. New York City contributed $288 million, and almost the entire balance—more than $2.1 billion—came from Washington. The federal Department of Housing and Urban Development also gives NYCHA hundreds of millions of dollars annually for capital uses, including replacing equipment and fixing roofs. It's hardly credible for de Blasio to accuse Washington of "systematic disinvestment" when the feds provide 60 percent of NYCHA's day-to-day budget—and have done so for decades.

In the 1930s, New York was especially aggressive about building public housing with local and state funding, in many cases ahead of federal financing. But the original intent of public housing in America was never, as de Blasio seems to believe, to build permanently subsidized apartments for poor people to inhabit for generations. In fact, the goal was something like the opposite: to use federal loan guarantees to erect the buildings and then fund their continuing operations through the rents of working- and middle-class occupants. Rents would cover costs and maintenance. The absence of landlords sucking profit out of their tenants would make public housing a desirable, self-sustaining option.

Through the late 1960s, NYCHA accepted tenants only if they had enough income to pay the rent and scrupulously evaluated applicants based on "social desirability," frequently evicting residents on moral grounds. But political pressure forced the agency to transition from providing "model housing" for aspirational families to "welfare housing" for the very poor. Urban decline and the rise of the suburbs led many middle-class families, including many NYCHA residents, to seek greener pastures.

Contrary to de Blasio's assertion that the "physical decline of NYCHA dates to 1980," officials identified major problems as early as the Preusse Report in 1957, which documented significant disrepair and "real obsolescence" at many projects. Broken glass and malfunctioning elevators, for example, have been a feature of NYCHA life for more than half a century. Crime has also been a persistent concern. Drug injection in the stairways and on roofs was noted as a problem as far back as 1959, and by 1971, the homicide rate in

NYCHA properties was rising at 10 times the overall city rate. Criminal complaints increased 170 percent from 1966 to 1971—a rate even more extraordinary when one considers that NYCHA has almost no commercial establishments.

As New York City edged toward bankruptcy in the 1970s, Washington assumed additional funding responsibilities for public housing. By then, federal policymakers had changed their priorities from building massive developments like NYCHA to offering programs such as Section 8 vouchers, established in 1974, which gave poor people direct federal subsidies to find housing in the private rental market.

Those who accept de Blasio's historical narrative point to how Reagan's HUD scaled back federal support that had helped public housing authorities close funding gaps. Yet even had Reagan increased support at the same levels, poor management and lax labor relations would have outpaced federal assistance. NYCHA's 2006 proposed budget complains that while Congress had appropriated a 4.6 percent increase in operating revenue in the previous year, "pension costs have increased 752 percent" and "collective bargaining agreements have increased labor costs 29 percent." The city was simply unable to control labor costs, which quickly devoured any increase in federal aid.

De Blasio's version of history is conveniently in line with his larger political beliefs. He takes it for granted that the federal government has primary responsibility for housing 400,000 New Yorkers. When those accommodations are as riddled with decay and disorder as NYCHA is, he can readily blame the feds. But it's decisions and failures made in

New York, largely based around collective-bargaining agreements, that are most responsible for NYCHA's predicament.

We see the same problem up and down throughout New York City government. Mayor de Blasio has been especially reckless in spending and hiring. When he came into office in 2014, the city budget was about $72 billion; the 2020 budget, the last before the pandemic, was $92.5 billion, modified upward to $94.4 billion in late 2019. This 28 percent increase in spending was roughly three times greater than the rate of inflation, a remarkable rise when you consider that most municipalities across the country have only recently returned to their pre-2008 recession levels.

New York City had a remarkable run after the recession. It was not hit so hard to begin with, and a substantial amount of the 2008–2009 bailouts, after all, went to support the financial industry, headquartered in Manhattan: one recalls that even after AIG was bought by the federal government, the managers responsible for the insurance giant's terrible investment parlays still received big bonuses. Bloomberg, for his part, immediately tightened the city's budget and reduced municipal employment by close to 6 percent, mainly through natural attrition, but including some layoffs.

The financial industry, still the core of New York City's prosperity, boomed through the 2010s. Wall Street employs about 5 percent of the private-sector workplace but accounts for 20 percent of wages. The stock market having increased about 85 percent just since de Blasio took over, the city's coffers ran over. These fat times coincided with the Progressive takeover of government, making for a kind of perfect storm:

excess revenue, a pathological drive to spend it, and no one there to put the brakes on.

De Blasio, enabled by a Progressive city council and an ambitious Progressive comptroller, contrived to spend every dime he could grab. When revenue outpaced expectations, the city would revise the budget upward at midyear to spend more. Hence, before the pandemic and the attendant fiscal crunch, Mayor de Blasio and the city council never had to budget, in the sense of choosing between competing priorities or cutting back on luxuries. They simply funded everything they could think of and created new "baselined" programs that were henceforth permanent.

Upon taking office, de Blasio moved immediately to reward political supporters. The United Federation of Teachers (UFT) was at the top of the list. Enmeshed in contract disputes with Bloomberg, who wanted the teachers to offer flexibility about work rules in exchange for hefty raises, the UFT decided to wait him out. They were smart: de Blasio gave them everything they wanted, including two retroactive 4 percent raises and an additional salary bump, in exchange for vaporous promises of healthcare savings that never materialized. The $3.6 billion price tag was so enormous that it had to be parceled out over the next seven years, with a final $1 billion disbursement—for work done more than a decade before—scheduled for October 2020.

When the time for the scheduled payout came due, the city was in the middle of its worst fiscal crisis since the 1970s. De Blasio indicated that he would forestall the payment, and the UFT immediately headed to arbitration. The administration settled on unfavorable terms: half the payout could be delayed for eight months, but with the proviso that there could be no layoffs, possibly past the end of de Blasio's term in office. This is a typical de Blasio move: he has no idea what the fiscal situation will be after he leaves, but he has saddled his successor with irresponsible conditions on labor relations.

Upon the urging of Al Sharpton, whom the mayor called "a blessing for this city," de Blasio upon taking office quickly settled a long-standing civil suit brought by the so-called Central Park Five, formerly known as the perpetrators of the 1989 night of mayhem in which, among other victims, the Central Park jogger had been raped and left to die. The five men, who confessed to the crime, had their convictions vacated in 2002 after a separate individual, already in prison for a different rape and murder and who left DNA at the scene, attested to his sole participation in the attack on the jogger. The Central Park Five sued the city in federal court in 2003; the Bloomberg administration fought the suit because there was no evidence of wrongdoing on the part of the city or the police.

In explaining why New York was reversing course and settling the suit, Zachary Carter, de Blasio's corporation counsel, refused to accept culpability by the NYPD but conceded that "we have determined that a resolution of this matter is in the best interests of the city." The mayor signed off on a $41 million payout, which Al Sharpton celebrated as a "monumental victory" for the Five and also a sign that he was "on the right side of history." In 2019, the group settled a separate lawsuit against New York State for the relatively paltry sum of $3.9 million.

De Blasio also settled an old lawsuit by black firemen alleging racial discrimination in the Fire Department of the City of New York (FDNY). The Bloomberg administration fought a seven-year legal battle against the Bush Justice Department, refusing to accept a stipulation that the city had "intentionally" engineered African American and Hispanic under-representation in the FDNY. But thanks to de Blasio's decision to settle the suit, taxpayers had to cough up close to $100 million in "broad injunctive relief and back pay."

When the Vulcan Society, the FDNY's black firefighters association, filed its first complaint against the city in 2002, few minorities worked in the fire department. At the time, African Americans constituted 25.6 percent of the population of New York City but only 3.4 percent of the FDNY—a statistic often cited as prima facie evidence of discriminatory hiring practices. Less remarked upon is the *over*representation of African Americans in other city agencies. In the Department of Corrections, for instance, 61 percent of personnel are African American and 18 percent are Latino. Corrections officers are paid at virtually the same scale as firefighters, so there is no economic reason for the discrepancy.

It's natural to wonder about a test that could produce such skewed results and that a federal judge ruled had "discriminatory effects on certain minority applicants, including black applicants, and failed to test for relevant job skills." If the test was intentionally designed to flunk minorities, surely it must have contained absurdly particularized questions meant to screen applicants on cultural knowledge or exclusionary questions such as might have been found at a Jim Crow–era poll site. The tests were culturally neutral, however. The math and reading-comprehension questions required some technical knowledge about firefighting. Some questions used diagrams and pictures to gauge applicants' ability to perform spatial translations or visualize a particular scene from a different angle.

The Vulcan Society's complaint was essentially that the test's emphasis on reading comprehension wasn't fair because fires are not extinguished by reading. The test, according to the Center for Constitutional Rights, which represented the Vulcan Society, "has no valid relationship to job skills"—a claim that the Department of Justice supported and which is necessary under Title VII of the Civil Rights Act to demonstrate unlawful discrimination. By the same logic, one infers, medical board exams should not involve a written exam because writing is secondary to the practice of medicine.

If African American and Hispanic applicants had done well on the FDNY exam, then there would likely be no dispute about its inherent racism. The only problem with the tests was their results, which retrospectively established bias in the eyes of the courts and, it seems, Mayor de Blasio. According to the logic of disparate impact, it doesn't matter whether the test seemed fair; its outcome proves that it was biased. In the realm of adverse effect, testing takes on a quantum aspect akin to the Schrödinger's cat paradox: you can't know whether the test is racist or not until you grade it.

Forgoing further appeals, de Blasio decided to settle with the Vulcan Society. The city agreed to disburse $99 million to black and Hispanic plaintiffs who failed the FDNY entrance exams in 1999 and 2002. According to the court's terms, African Americans who scored at least 25 percent on the exams (applicants needed to score 70 percent to pass) became eligible for back pay and fringe benefits, as well as preference in hiring and promotion.

Not a bad deal: fail a civil service exam abysmally, go back to whatever you were doing previously, and then 10 years later get a check for years of back pay for work you were never hired to do.

These were headline-worthy onetime expenses but amount to peanuts in the context of the close to $100 billion in excess spending—that is, new spending over the inflation rate—that the 2014 Progressive Ascendency effected. "New York Works" was supposed to create 100,000 "good-paying jobs." After shelling out $300 million, the program can point to 3,000 jobs that can—perhaps—be credited to its efforts. De Blasio reversed Michael Bloomberg's policy of shuttering failing schools, instead vowing to turn them around. Consisting of intensive resource allocation—including, in some cases, the installation of laundry facilities so that parents would have a convenient place to wash the family's clothes—the Renewal Schools program soaked up $750 million before the mayor announced that it hadn't worked.

New York City Health + Hospitals (H+H) is the nation's largest public hospital network, and it provides primary and critical care to hundreds of thousands of residents, regardless of ability to pay. The network's budget is almost $8 billion annually; much of this is met through insurance, including substantial federal assistance. Nonetheless, H+H runs a significant deficit every year, requiring the city's taxpayers to kick in money to keep the doors open. City support in 2009 was $359 million but rose to $1.7 billion by 2019. By 2023, the city is expected to have to pay $2.3 billion in extra subsidies to keep its public hospitals and clinics running.

Why is a world-class public hospital system accruing so much debt every year? New York City has approximately 800,000 illegal aliens whose medical care is nonreimbursable by the federal government; nearly 100 percent of the cost of their care falls on the city's taxpayers. In 2016, Ram Raju, the president of the hospital system, estimated that fully one-third of its total budget goes to care for undocumented immigrants. Thus New York City spends almost $3 billion, every year, for healthcare for illegal aliens—a direct result of the "sanctuary city" policy that enforces resolutely a see-no-evil approach to immigration status. If this money were used to borrow money for capital projects, it could easily fund $100 billion in capital expenditure bonds—enough to fix the subways, public housing, and the city's crumbling highways and leave over a hefty sum for other important projects.

The list goes on and on: the expansion of the mayor's senior staff, with dozens of "special assistants" making six-figure salaries; $100 million a year to advertise the availability of primary care clinics to illegal immigrants; the addition of thousands of new vehicles to the city's fleet; and the provision of free lawyers for people fighting deportation cases in regional detention facilities, many of whom don't even live in New York City. The mayor assigned a full-time videographer to work exclusively for his wife. In December 2020, Chirlane McCray debuted a video of herself dancing to Sister Sledge's 1979 hit song "We Are Family" on the steps of Gracie Mansion. The videographer, who earned $77,000 annually, was one of 14 city workers on McCray's staff.

The greatest expansion of New York City spending under Progressive rule is the municipal workforce, which grew from fewer than 300,000 employees when the mayor took over to almost 334,000 in 2020, an increase of 11 percent. All this hiring, according to a spokesperson from the mayor's office, "reflects an increase in the level of quality services New Yorkers need and expect, and has propelled our students to success."

The correlation between more workers and a higher "level of quality services" seems dubious. The Department of Corrections' headcount went up 17 percent, for instance, even as violence in the jail system soared. To be sure, thousands of teachers were added to the employment rolls to handle the expansion of universal prekindergarten, but the administration increased nonpedagogical employment at the Department of Education by 2,500, or roughly 11 percent, including hundreds of high-paying administrative roles with the central office. Chancellor Richard Carranza hired a number of former staffers from his previous positions at salaries near or above $200,000 to fill newly created positions.

Expanding municipal employment raises the operational cost of government. But it also feeds a much larger problem, which is a $200 billion pension and benefits bomb, most of which is an "unfunded liability" that hangs over New York City.

Municipal workers in New York have access to a generous pension program, which kicks in, for some workers, after as few as 10 years of service. These pensions pay out a percentage of the employee's salary for life and are a vestige of the days when American workers—in the private and public sectors—relied on pensions from their employers for their retirement. Those were the years when people expected to have the same job for decades, retire at age 65, and die shortly thereafter. Investing in the stock market was for the rich.

In the last 40 years, the old employer pension model of retirement has largely faded. Most workers engage in portable workplace-based direct contribution systems, like the 401(k), where they and their employer direct a portion of their salary toward a privately managed retirement account invested in stocks, bonds, and other assets. But many large municipalities like New York City still cling to the old pension model, to which, by federal law, the local government is required to contribute money every year, to a dedicated fiduciary fund, to cover anticipated future payments. This annual amount is tied to market performance but currently totals about $9.5 billion, or 11 percent of the entire city budget.

The real problem, the elephant in the coffee cup, is the nonpension lifetime benefits that the city has promised to cover for its workers. Unlike most employers, New York provides its workers with totally free healthcare and extends that coverage to its retired workers and their spouses until death. After they reach age 65, these retirees go on Medicare, and the city picks up the cost of their supplemental coverage and Part B reimbursement, too. There are no federal fiduciary laws regarding prefunding this debt; the city just pays as it goes. The cost just for future retiree healthcare costs is estimated at $100 billion and is growing rapidly. Current outlays run about $4.8 billion annually.

Public pensions for work that has already been performed are constitutionally guaranteed in New York State and can't be altered or amended. But that's not the case for retiree health benefits, which are just a perk. So what's to stop New York City from just sending out a letter advising everyone that they will have to start chipping in to cover their insurance premiums, like everyone else does?

The problem is the overwhelming power of public-sector unions, which dominate New York politics more than any other single force and which would fight any diminution of their benefits ferociously. Most people, when they think of unions, think of hardworking people who come together to bargain collectively against an employer who seeks to exploit their labor to squeeze out more profit for himself or herself and the other owners of the enterprise. Indeed, this is still the image that today's government worker unions promote to their members and the public at large.

It's an image affirmed and amplified by Bill de Blasio. When the ability of public-sector unions to force nonmembers to pay fees was under threat in a major Supreme Court case, the mayor stood firm—for the unions. He announced

New York City is the city it is today because of the hardworking unionized men and women who built it and run it. Our city is stronger because of unions' ability to organize and fight for all of our rights. Especially in the face of our current political climate, we should be bolstering tools for empowering and protecting workers not making them more difficult to come by.

Here we see an essential contradiction in the role of the public-sector union, which aptly demonstrates the difference between government-employee unions and unions in the private sector. In the private sector, the workers bargain with management, which is appointed by the owners of the enterprise. Management is tasked with controlling costs—including the cost of labor—in order to maximize the return on the investors' capital, otherwise called profit. Labor and management have shared interests, but they are also in direct competition with each other.

But in the public sector, where is the profit that the owners are trying to squeeze out of the workers? Who are the shareholders of the New York City Department of Sanitation? Management in the public sector is the government, which represents the people, who are the ultimate bosses of public employees. In private industry, the workers are paid through the sale of goods and services they have a role in producing. But in the public sector, government workers are paid by taxes, most of which derive from people who work in the private sector. In a manner of speaking, that is not as unfair as it sounds: government workers don't pay taxes—they are paid by taxes.

Moreover, unions are major donors in the political process, and big-city politicians jockey to serve them. Thus unions essentially pick their bosses, which leads to a significant conflict of interest. De Blasio's hero, Franklin D. Roosevelt, made this point explicitly in 1937, just two years after workers had gained the right to organize into unions and bargain collectively. In a letter to the head of the federal workers' association, FDR acknowledged that while government employees had legitimate concerns, "meticulous attention should be paid to the special relationships and obligations of public servants to the public itself and to the Government."

FDR explained

> that the process of collective bargaining, as usually understood, cannot be transplanted into the public service. It has its distinct and insurmountable limitations when applied to public personnel management. The very nature and purposes of Government make it impossible for administrative officials to represent fully or to bind the employer in mutual discussions with Government employee organizations. The employer is the whole people, who speak by means of laws enacted by their representatives in Congress.

To this day, federal workers do not have the right to bargain collectively. But, starting in the late 1950s, many cities and states began to recognize bargaining units among their employees. New York City led the way in this movement, at a time when close to a third of all workers nationally belonged to a union, virtually all of them in private enterprise; the rate was higher in New York. Sixty years later, 37 percent of public-sector workers belong to a union versus only 6.4 percent of workers in private industry.

Organized labor no longer has the numbers or the power to bring the nation to a standstill by calling strikes in coal mines, railroads, or factories. But public, employee unions exercise even greater power such that they almost never have to strike to get what they want. Fattened on dues that workers were obligated to pay for decades, whether they were members or not, public-sector unions have been able to mold local government into an instrument whose purpose is to satisfy union demands.

In New York City, 69 percent of public-sector employees belong to a union. Counted separately, but working toward similar ends, healthcare workers—whose salaries depend enormously on state funding—represent a large constituency, too. These organizations represent hundreds of thousands of votes and millions of dollars in political contributions. Union locals occupy hundreds of staffers, organizers, and political operatives, many of whom have never worked in the union's underlying trade but whose job is to keep pressure on elected officials, liaise with community groups, and behave as full-time political activists. Public-sector unions may sometimes have divergent local aims, but preservation of retiree pension and healthcare benefits is always the key goal.

What New York City faces is a cadre of government employees who have taken control of local government and whose power is virtually unquestioned. Out of approximately 150 elected local, state, and national officials from New York City, one could count on one hand the number who take seriously the fact that paying for lifetime healthcare for hundreds of thousands of municipal retirees will bankrupt New York City while squeezing out spending on schools and other services.

In the spring of 2020, as the city faced a massive decline in revenue and a $10 billion deficit, Mayor de Blasio began to warn that layoffs of municipal workers were a looming possibility. For months he demanded an immediate federal bailout to "make us whole," or else layoffs would ensue. In April he reported

the one thing that I've asked the President for lately that should be the easiest part of the equation is to help New York City through this crisis, give us the financial support to make us whole, to actually balance our budget, pay our first responders and our public servants who are doing this work.

In October, by which time it became clear that Washington would not rush to bail out cities that were both financially irresponsible and dragging their heels in reopening their local economies, de Blasio returned to his old theme, saying, "It is time for higher taxes on millionaires and billionaires. I think absolutely the stock transfer tax has to be reassessed now because it's unbelievable that, you know, there's threats of layoffs to tens of thousands of working people."

De Blasio's constant threats to lay off city employees were presumably intended to shock the conscience of the nation and goad local New Yorkers into fury. But workers in New York's private sector were already suffering from mass unemployment themselves. Even at the end of October, New York City's unemployment rate was double the rest of the nation, with one million people out of work. Why would lifetime job protection for municipal workers be the main priority for city taxpayers? The tourism, theater, and restaurant industries were devastated. Not that anyone wanted to see government workers lose their jobs, too, but de Blasio's assumption—that New Yorkers would sooner die than see some municipal employees get laid off in a major fiscal crisis—affirmed again what close observers already knew: public-sector employees, along with other members of the donor class, are the real constituency of New York's elected officials.

· · · · · · · · · ·

The primary obsession of all Progressives is wealth and income inequality, which is to say racial disparities in who has more wealth and income. Inequality is basically a proxy for talking about how unfair things are for nonwhites. If blacks and Latinos had more money than white people, it is unlikely that wealth and income inequality would be such an important topic. There is no discussion of public policy that does not include a focus on inequality. In fact, it is fair to say that tackling inequality, in a city run by the Prog, *is* public policy. Any policy that is not dedicated to eliminating inequality, by definition, reinforces existing structures of inequality.

Bill de Blasio has run his entire career talking about wealth and income inequality. His original campaign slogan regarding the "tale of two cities" was premised on the idea that the haves and have-nots of New York are in a kind of war. It's the foundational myth of all leftist economics that wealth is theft and that principle—usually stated less bluntly but there nevertheless—underwrites the Progressive idea of how to fix society. De Blasio made this point at his first budget-related press conference, in February of 2014, when he announced, "we are beginning to implement my progressive agenda for New York City."

He then presented a chart to demonstrate the emergency New York faced.

> Now, let's look—we've talked a lot about inequality in the city and in this country—let's look at the numbers because they're quite shocking. Income inequality in the United States at levels not seen since the 1920s. You can see this here—the last peaks of this level literally at the dawn of the Great Depression. New York City? An even starker situation. The percentage of income earned by the top one percent of earners in the United States of America around 20 percent. In New York City, in the high 30s—almost twice as much.

This "stark" situation sounds really bad, if you assume that income inequality is a major problem. But as fiscal expert Nicole Gelinas has noted,

> the fact that New York remains home to so many fabulously rich people hasn't been a bad thing for the city's poor. For it is Gotham's vast private wealth that disproportionately pays for the city's vast *public* wealth, including mass transit, museums, libraries, and public parks.

Income inequality is not a bug of city life—it's a feature.

New York City is a magnet for people from all over the world who flock here in order to—in the classic formulation—"seek a better life." Immigrants from abroad comprise almost 40 percent of the city's entire population. But these strivers don't come because of the promise of *equality*. The attraction is opportunity, the promise that working hard will pay off in the form of upward mobility. Despite the Progressive narrative of New York as a place of misery and despair, where the super-rich make almost 40 percent of all the income, New York City is one of the most economically mobile cities in the country. Ten percent of people born in the bottom fifth of the economic ladder in New York City will wind up in the top fifth; that makes New York the sixth best city in the country for improving one's lot in life economically.

To get the Progressive agenda rolling, the mayor and his obedient city council enacted a series of laws to expand rights and benefits for workers, including paid sick leave, new rules on scheduling, and outlawing the use of criminal checks for hiring. The city also prohibited most employers from using prehiring drug tests for marijuana as a condition for employment and imposed new regulations on employers of freelancers.

The mayor and his Progressive allies spoke about the expansion of paid sick leave as an unalloyed victory for progress. "This is going to be one city, where everyone has a shot and rises together," said de Blasio. "This is the culmination of a movement and coalition that has put the rights and needs of families at the center of our agenda," announced then council speaker Melissa Mark-Viverito. "Mayor de Blasio and Speaker Mark-Viverito are ushering in a new progressive era by reinvigorating our social safety net," toasted Congresswoman Nydia Velázquez.

Among the huzzahs and congratulations, not a word was heard about the businesses that would shoulder the financial burden of providing an extra paid week annually per employee—not to mention the administrative costs of recordkeeping, rolling over unused hours, and the like. For major companies with dedicated human resource departments, these functions are built in, but for a small family restaurant, it's a different story. Indeed, many of the achievements that the Progressive ascendancy has touted and celebrated as part of making New York the "fairest big city in the nation" are really just new requirements on small businesses.

It may be that the social importance of paid sick leave outweighs the petty bookkeeping concerns of the city's small businesses—but imagine how galling it must be for a shopkeeper to hear elected officials take credit for something that, after all, they are strong-arming other people to do. When Progressives expand the regulatory framework in which businesses operate, they claim credit for taking bold steps to fix social ills—but they also create consequences that they will never have to deal with themselves.

In his battle to out-Progressive de Blasio, Governor Cuomo hiked the minimum wage to $15 per hour—and cast the move in reverential terms as the "Mario Cuomo Campaign for Economic Justice" (named after his late father, the former governor). The state government website describes the rise in the pay floor as "one of the single-most progressive actions to help working families."

A higher minimum wage, along with the various protections and benefits that the Progressives have implemented, may be a net positive. Probably there are low-income workers whose lives have been made easier because of the new regulations. But as economist Thomas Sowell has observed about the minimum wage, "Unfortunately, the real minimum wage is always zero, regardless of the laws, and that is the wage that many workers receive in the wake of the creation or escalation of a government-mandated minimum wage, because they lose their jobs or fail to find jobs when they enter the labor force." Minimum wages make it harder for young, unskilled workers to get hired simply because they don't produce enough value to make it worth hiring them at a mandatorily higher rate.

It's one thing to impose higher wages and extensive employment regulations on businesses when the economy is booming and employers have to compete for quality workers. But what about when a recession hits? That's what happened in 2020, when New York City's restaurants, nail salons, and many other businesses were forced to close because of the COVID-19 pandemic. Smaller, undercapitalized businesses survive on tiny profit margins even when times are flush.

As the city economy began to reopen, businesses were hammered by having to meet the inflexibly narrow Progressive labor regulations, which fine chain restaurants for changing employees' schedules without giving them 72 hours' notice. This is all in addition to the fines that restaurants may face, from seven different city agencies, for dozens of infractions regarding everything from improperly keeping a delivery-food bicycle roster to failure to post a refund policy to failure to clean 18 inches into the street. But the Progressive leadership could only shake its collective head and wonder why the unemployment rate remained so high.

Just as the Progressives outsourced the implementation of their agenda to the private sector, organized labor put the onus of organizing workers on government. Not every industry is as easy to unionize as the public sector, where "management" is pliable and does the bidding of the unions. And with major manufacturing having largely fled New York City for friendlier climes, unions have to dig into obscure corners of the labor market to find new members. An unusual 2015 law, the Car Wash Accountability Act, forced all car washes in the city to carry a bond ensuring that their workers would be paid in the event of a wage dispute. Car wash owners had to buy a $150,000 bond—unless they had a unionized workforce, in which case the required bond was only $30,000.

By imposing such a significant penalty on nonunion car washes, the Progressives in City Hall were effectively compelling these small, independent businesses to unionize their own workforces. Extensive federal law regarding how workers form unions includes no mechanism for localities to impose unionization on businesses, though, and a federal judge initially ruled that the Car Wash Accountability Act violates the National Labor Relations Act, noting, "pressuring businesses to unionize is impermissible under the NLRA, as it inserts the City directly into labor-management bargaining."

The Car Wash Accountability Act did not originate in the city council but as a legislative reaction to a long, mostly failed effort on the part of organized labor and immigrant activist groups to unionize these businesses. Starting in 2012, the Retail, Wholesale, and Department Store Union (RWDSU) began a push to organize New York City's 200 car washes, which mostly employ low-skilled illegal immigrants. The effort has not succeeded: at one point, 10 car washes had been unionized, but several have reportedly gone out of business since then.

The problem is that car washes are independently owned small businesses that can easily replace their workforce with machines. In most parts of the country, car washes are largely automated and operate with just a few workers; the New York City model of having a team of *carwasheros* buffing and scrubbing each car is mostly a function of the low cost of local immigrant labor. Organizing shop by shop is an intensive, expensive operation, so the RWDSU, which contributes mightily to political campaigns, took a shortcut to mass unionization—which could require professional "organizers" to take difficult jobs at car washes and win the trust and backing of their fellow workers—by having the city council and mayor legislate it into effect.

With brick-and-mortar retail cratering nationwide, it's hard to imagine a rosy future for the RWDSU. A 2014 *New York Times* article extolled the steady work schedules and guaranteed minimum hours of unionized employees at Macy's flagship Herald Square location. In 2016, 5,000 Macy's employees authorized a strike, and local elected officials, including Mayor de Blasio, joined the battle to force the company to agree to higher wages and other demands, averting labor action. In 2017, Macy's announced plans to close at least 100 stores and lay off 10,000 employees. In 2020, the Herald Square flagship store was looted during the George Floyd riots, and the fabled chain hovered on the brink of bankruptcy.

With the Internet depriving organized labor of new retail workers to organize, unions such as the RWDSU and SEIU have turned to nontraditional employees—like the *carwasheros*—as potential new members. Fast-food restaurants emerged as another prime opportunity for organizing, but unions have made little headway in getting burger flippers to sign up. A large percentage of these workers are young people working their first job: in New York State, 23.4 percent of fast-food employees have not completed high school, and 28.4 percent are 21 or younger. As a point of comparison, only 6.1 percent of New York State's overall workforce is in the same age bracket, indicating that fast-food employment is indeed a stepping stone into the workforce and not viewed by most younger workers as a lifetime career demanding union protection.

Further, despite bearing the names and logos of international corporations, most fast-food restaurants are franchises operated as small to medium-size businesses. Unionizing these companies means going shop by shop and painstakingly organizing a transient, young workforce. Or failing that, going to the city council with a set of bills that would impose—just on one industry—all the conditions that would normally be included in a collective-bargaining agreement.

The "Fair Work Week" legislative package, signed by the mayor at the end of May 2020, imposes wide-ranging rules on scheduling, forcing fast-food restaurants to set schedules 14 days in advance and penalizing management if changes are made within that period. The package also limits businesses from hiring new workers before offering existing staff the opportunity to absorb additional hours. Both of these conditions are typical of unionized shops, especially the latter, which will effectively force employers to maintain a leaner workforce, inevitably leading to payment of overtime.

Another law in the Fair Work Week package allows fast-food workers to authorize their employers to deduct money from their paychecks and direct the money to "nonprofit organizations of their choice." Labor unions and "employee organizations" are not permitted to receive these contributions; however, allied radical organizations such as New York Communities for Change (the successor organization to ACORN) or Make the Road (an illegal immigrant advocacy group) are eligible.

Nevertheless, the activist legislation is ultimately as unlikely to benefit fast-food workers as the earlier law did car wash workers. Both industries are easily subject to automation and are beginning to build in the mechanical or digital infrastructure that will render low-skilled workers superfluous. Government can take the side of organized labor and act as its agent when labor fails to organize, but businesses cannot be compelled to hire workers above their value.

The Car Wash Accountability Act was upheld by the courts, to the jubilation of the elected Progressives and their friends in organized labor and the professional activist class. As a predictable result, many car washes have closed, and others have become automated. Now, entrepreneurial out-of-work *carwasheros* have set up sidewalk car washes out of vans on nonresidential streets of Upper Manhattan, undercutting the bonded, legitimate car wash businesses that can no longer afford to hire them. With no understanding of how businesses work or the role of supply and demand in the labor market, Progressives try to engineer reality to meet their ideals. Unfortunately, reality has a way of puncturing even the dreamiest utopian bubbles.

Hassling small business is business as usual for the urban Democratic left. But there's always been, essentially, a recognition that the modern municipal welfare state requires the presence of—and tacit toleration for—corporate America to have a tax base to pay for social programs. This consensus was shattered in late 2018 with the news that Amazon—the nation's largest retailer—planned to site a major office in western Queens, bringing at least 25,000 well-paying corporate jobs to New York City and investing billions more in building its East Coast headquarters.

This announcement, made just a few weeks following the "Blue Wave" that confirmed the victory of socialist darling Alexandria Ocasio-Cortez (AOC), along with a number of downballot fellow travelers, was met with howls of scorn and anger by local politicians and activists, who condemned a deal that would offer Amazon some $3 billion in combined state and local subsidies as "massive corporate welfare from scarce public resources."

Giving public subsidies to private corporations to encourage them to relocate is bad policy. It encourages a race to the bottom between jurisdictions and rarely delivers promised results. But the Amazon deal was not a good example of a corporate giveaway. The deal would have offered $3 billion in state tax credits and abatements, much of which any job-creating company would be legally entitled to, in any event, stretched over at least 15 or 20 years. That amounts to about $200 million annually, on the high side.

The combined budget of New York City and State for 2019 was roughly $235 billion. As a point of reference, in 2016 the city paid out $1.7 billion just in overtime. The Amazon package, in the context of city and state spending that will amount to trillions of dollars over the course of the next decade, is a rounding error. Moreover, the money was not, as opponents would have it, being "stolen" from New Yorkers, because it represented foregone taxes on income that wouldn't exist if Amazon didn't move here.

Meanwhile, politicians who bitterly condemned the Amazon deal as a "scam" or "giveaway" are hard to take seriously because New York routinely disburses billions of dollars every year in economic development money, with far less transparent results, and no one except cranky fiscal conservatives ever makes a fuss about it. The difference is that most of that money is dispensed to favored constituents. The Amazon deal was worked out behind closed doors between Governor Cuomo, Mayor de Blasio, and Jeff Bezos—the local pols were shut out, which left them red-faced, fuming, and anxious to gain political advantage.

After several months of protests, lawsuits, and legislative maneuverings to block the deal, Amazon gave up and decided there were friendlier places to set up shop—cities that would welcome 25,000 high-paying jobs and the corresponding development of building a major corporate headquarters. But the Democrat socialist left, led by AOC, was ecstatic. "Today was the day a group of dedicated, everyday New Yorkers and their neighbors defeated Amazon's corporate greed, its worker exploitation and the power of the richest man in the world," she tweeted.

Ocasio-Cortez also celebrated the evaporation of the Amazon deal by broadcasting her economic illiteracy. "Frankly, if we were willing to give away $3 billion for this deal," she explained, "we could invest those $3 billion in our district, ourselves, if we wanted to. We could hire out more teachers. We can fix our subways. We can put a lot of people to work for that amount of money if we wanted to." But the $3 billion was never a bag of money that the city and state were going to hand to Amazon: it was just credit against future obligations, which would now never be incurred. The Progressive belief that wealth is theft and that capitalism is zero-sum is made manifest in AOC's illogic about the bag of magical beans that she can now plant to grow schools and subway cars.

Even in 2019, New York State could ill afford to thumb its nose at 25,000 well-paying jobs, which would have produced billions of dollars in tax revenues and contributed mightily to the local economy. Following the collapse of local tax revenues and the continued loss of residents to less fractious and expensive jurisdictions, the opposition to Amazon seems more than ever like opportunity lost. Critics of the plan can rejoice in their success in having prevented economic development in a moribund area of western Queens. They have preserved stagnation and called it progress.

· · · · · · · · · ·

The Progressive war on business reached a kind of comic apogee in early 2018 when Mayor de Blasio announced that he would sue the entire oil industry, seeking unspecified damages, but certainly amounting to tens of billions of dollars. The immediate cause for the suit, filed against BP, Chevron, ConocoPhillips, ExxonMobil, and Shell, is the damage and expenses associated with climate change— caused by the oil companies. In particular, the city wants to recoup the costs of rebuilding from Superstorm Sandy in 2011 and the $20 billion that it plans to spend on storm resiliency. The fossil fuel energy industry, the city's lawsuit claims, "deliberately engaged in a campaign of deception and denial about global warming and its impacts, even while profiting from the sale of fossil fuels."

Asked about the litigation strategy, de Blasio dismissed the suggestion that it might be hard to prove that the defendants literally caused the hurricane. "I think we are going to win the argument that climate change exists; I feel really confident about that one," he chuckled. "And I think it's pretty clear these five companies had something to do with it." New York City corporation counsel Zachary Carter described the case as a straightforward tort action, based on damages from Sandy.

"The theory of this lawsuit," explained Carter, "is it exploits our nuisance laws, and that both in terms of public and private nuisance we believe that's a cause of action that . . . gives us certain strategic advantages in litigation." The $200 billion multistate tobacco industry settlement, reached in 1998, is the model for the city's litigation, said the mayor. "The tobacco analogy is important," he observed, explaining that a cultural change occurred after "Big Tobacco" admitted to having buried evidence that cigarette use is unhealthy. "We no longer assume that the fossil fuel companies are innocent; in fact, if we identify them as guilty, it changes the reality . . . and that can spread like wildfire."

But the analogy between the tobacco and fossil fuel industries is misleading. Cigarette companies did conduct research on their proprietary tobacco formulations; the findings indicated that smoking had negative health ramifications on their consumers. The companies did suppress or distort their discoveries that smoking causes lung cancer and emphysema. A case can be made that the tobacco companies defrauded individual smokers by addicting them to a deadly product while lying about its safety.

Energy companies, in contrast, sell a product that was an integral element of the historical epoch called the Industrial Age, which has seen the world's productive capacity expand by multiple orders of magnitude since 1850 and in which billions of people have been eager participants. Fossil fuels permeate every aspect of society, from transportation to manufacturing to food production; whatever our hopes for a green future, modern life for the past 150 years is unthinkable without oil, gas, and coal.

De Blasio put on an air of total confidence about this cockamamie idea, which was in retrospect just a stunt for his coming presidential run and which was dismissed by a judge six months later. But when a reporter asked if he would cut back his frequent use of SUVs to shuttle him to Brooklyn for his daily workouts at the Park Slope YMCA, his answer was instructive in how deeply it betrayed Progressive ignorance about energy and how we use it.

His convoy cars are hybrids, the mayor said, adding that the city is moving to replace its entire fleet of cars with electric vehicles, which emit no exhaust. Fair enough, but the electricity that powers those cars comes off the grid, and most of that electricity is still generated by oil, coal, and gas. The answer was typical Progressive showboating: gestures and virtue signaling preempt practical management or governance.

Never one to waste an opportunity to seize the means of production, Mayor de Blasio's first impulse when the pandemic hit in late winter 2020 was to demand that the federal government nationalize industry. When COVID-19 slammed New York in March 2020, everyone's major concern was that hospitals would run out of space, supplies, and equipment to treat seriously ill patients. It was as a logistical consideration, remember, that society was "locked down" to "flatten the curve" and dampen the exponential spread of contagion. The idea was to buy time to keep emergency rooms from being overrun. Only later did the concern shift to making sure that nobody ever became infected with the virus and that we all "stay safe."

Mayor de Blasio and Governor Cuomo initially dismissed the disease as a matter of minor concern to New York and criticized Donald Trump for restricting travel from China. But as critical care hospital admissions started to increase, doubling every few days, officials began to panic. New York City, it turned out, despite having preached preparedness after Superstorm Sandy killed dozens of New Yorkers and caused billions of dollars of damage, was largely unprepared for dealing with a pandemic, even one as relatively nonlethal as COVID-19. The city and state lacked even basic protective gear like gloves, masks, and hand sanitizer—though both de Blasio and Cuomo had waged public information emergency readiness campaigns urging New Yorkers to stock just those materials at home and in "Go Bags" in case of a disaster.

The mayor immediately demanded that the entire nation go on a "war footing" and got very excited and sentimental about it, the same way he gets enthusiastic about the Great Depression or other calamities, as an opportunity for everyone to pull together under the aegis of expanded government authority. De Blasio explained

> You know, I've said I grew up in a family that served in World War II—a lot of members of—my mom, my dad, a lot of members of my family served in the war effort. So, I actually got up hearing about what a fully mobilized society was like, where everyone had a common goal and everyone understood we're going to sacrifice, we're all going to have to pool the resources we have. This is the world we're going into now. The City's going to play a very aggressive role, but we absolutely need the federal government to get us on a war footing and a national mobilization.

A few weeks later, in early April, de Blasio penned an opinion piece in the *New York Times* that called upon "the federal government to enlist all doctors and health workers, and mobilize them in a way we've never seen . . . about a million doctors and 3.8 million nurses." As a point of comparison, the United States drafted only 2.2 million soldiers to fight the Vietnam War between 1964 and 1975.

"So many of us grew up hearing stories from our parents and grandparents about America in its toughest moments," the mayor rhapsodized in his opinion piece. "It is hard to believe our generation would face a challenge on the same scale. But that's exactly where we are. The next days and weeks will decide how we'll be remembered." De Blasio's grandiosity and thirst for "sacrifice"—from others, naturally—sounds rhetorically like Mussolini on an off day. De Blasio manifested, almost nakedly, Progressive "worsism." An old maxim, attributed to Lenin, goes, "The worse, the better," meaning that intensifying the misery of life under capitalism and bourgeois democracy will hasten revolutionary change. De Blasio thrills to the idea that "we're all going to have to pool the resources we have," because the fog and uncertainty of life only clear when misery settles upon the land and government is allowed to assume charge of things.

The lockdown was depressing and miserable for everyone. Stores closed, and it wasn't clear if they would ever open again. Hundreds of thousands of people left the city. Wealthier New Yorkers with second homes or the means to rent one went to Long Island, the Berkshires, or upstate. Young aspirants who came to New York for a few years as a sojourn—a post-college rite of passage in the big city—accelerated their return to wherever they came from or planned to go next. Mid-career professionals who found they could work remotely moved to Florida, North Carolina, or Vermont. The Black Lives Matter/Antifa riots and looting accentuated the sense that New York City was in decline. The storefronts and office buildings of Midtown Manhattan emptied.

Facing the possibly permanent disappearance of a large segment of the city's revenue-generating productive base, de Blasio assumed his characteristic posture of scorn toward

Manhattan. In response to an August 2020 *New York Times* article fretting over a lack of civic leadership, de Blasio's jejune press secretary tweeted, "The working people of NYC have a champion. The question everyone in this piece seems to be asking is 'what about the rich and the powerful???? What will we ever do?' Kick rocks, billionaires."

A few weeks later, in a radio interview, the mayor echoed his spokesman's sentiment, pleading with New Yorkers to embrace his radical vision of change. "What changes things is redistribution of wealth," he explained. "Tax the wealthy at a much higher level. . . . Help me tax the wealthy, help me redistribute wealth, help me build affordable housing in white communities."

In October, after Donald Trump said that New York City had become a ghost town, de Blasio disputed the idea that the city is defined by its core business district. He cited the success of outdoor dining as evidence that local communities were thriving. "There's a lot of vibrancy in neighborhoods. You got commercial strips all over the city, in the five boroughs you see a lot of activity." The importance of Midtown Manhattan, according to de Blasio, was overstated as a key to the continued prosperity of New York. "A lot of the business leaders think of the world from Midtown out. Midtown is a center of universe," the mayor opined. "I think it's the other way around. It's the five boroughs, it's where people live, it's communities, and then Midtown is important, but it's not the center of our universe."

It's fine to cop an attitude and tell billionaires—the segment of the population with the greatest opportunity for mobility and the most choices about where to live—to get stuffed when Manhattan is the most appealing place in the country. But when the main drivers of the city's revenue—income and property taxes—are in free fall, and when the tourism, entertainment, and hospitality industries have mostly evaporated, and farebox revenue on the nation's busiest transit system is at 10 percent of where it was, it seems perverse in the extreme to sneer at people who—like it or not—pay the bills.

It's worth remembering that the top 0.1 percent of high-income residents—the 3,500 people who make more than $5 million annually—pay almost one quarter of all New York City income tax. You don't have to be a bootlicking running dog of capitalism to recognize that encouraging all the rich people to "kick rocks" isn't a great plan for economic recovery.

And what was de Blasio's suggestion for economic recovery? Well, outdoor dining and letting retailers set up tables on the sidewalk were two solutions he offered, the latter coming just as the weather was turning nasty—these ideas let restaurants and small businesses scrape up some income but were hardly going to save the city. Fortunately, Bill de Blasio came up with a recovery agenda that "acknowledges the powerful link between the city's economic health and the health of New Yorkers."

"New York City is about to enter a transformational era," the mayor announced. The city's newfound expertise in tackling a pandemic was going to pay off handsomely, because New York was going to become the new national center for public health research.

We will make New York a center of innovation for public health research, design, and practice. We will build new research and development facilities and forge collaboration among unlikely partners—doctors and nurses, academic researchers, industry innovators, health nonprofits and economic development community organizations, just as we did in early days of COVID-19. Because health security depends upon a highly trained workforce, we will create a Public Health Corps—a team of community health workers building trust and taking care of people in our hardest hit neighborhoods.

The idea that being the place that was hardest hit by the pandemic in the country—largely because local and state government mismanaged the response—means that New York ought to retool its economy around public health sounds like a tasteless joke. It's like if someone told Dresden to leverage its expertise in rubble removal or suggested that Flint, Michigan, can become the headquarters of Pür water filters.

Moreover, public health research is not a money-making industry, which is why the federal government runs it; there's two cities, Bethesda and Atlanta, the homes of the National Institutes of Health (NIH) and the Centers for Disease Control and Prevention (CDC), that already handle America's public health research.

De Blasio's real "plan" for economic recovery and development, aside from waiting for a federal bailout, was the same plan that Progressives always offer: to tax the "millionaires and billionaires." But there's no way to ensure that the truly rich will hang around waiting to be eaten, so "millionaires and billionaires" is just code for "anybody with a job." That's the great thing about defining class war as between the 1 percent and the 99 percent: as the actual rich people leave, you can just bump the middle class into the top spot and tax them.

5

De Blasio's Bosses:
How Consultants Run the City

IN THE SUMMER OF 2013, Bill de Blasio's faltering mayoral campaign got a boost when he participated in a protest against the closure of a Brooklyn hospital and was arrested. The Long Island College Hospital (LICH), a long-time teaching hospital in Brooklyn, was bought by the State University of New York (SUNY) system in 2011. Like many hospitals statewide, LICH was losing money, costing the state $10 million a month in subsidies, and SUNY voted in 2013 to close it. Neighborhood activists protested that closing the hospital would have a negative effect on community health, that SUNY had misrepresented its purpose in buying LICH, and that there was a lack of clarity regarding the future of the site. But the main opponent of the closure was the immensely powerful healthcare workers union, 1199SEIU, which was backing de Blasio's run.

De Blasio made a speech at the demonstration and joined a dozen protestors in chanting "No hospital, no peace!" while they blocked the entrance to SUNY's main building on 42nd Street in Manhattan, before being handcuffed and led to the precinct, where they cooled their heels for less than two hours before being released. A month later, a judge ordered SUNY to resume health services at LICH. Advocates cheered the news. The arrest garnered de Blasio extensive press coverage and is credited with helping turn his mayoral campaign around.

Six months after taking office, Mayor de Blasio announced that a deal was in the works for LICH to be closed for good and the valuable site in Brooklyn Heights sold to a real estate development company for hundreds of millions of dollars. The mayor was pleased to report that as a result of his interventions, Fortis Property Group would include "affordable" units for low-income tenants in its plans, as well as a health clinic and other public amenities. 1199 SEIU, the union representing 1,200 LICH workers, and which had led the fierce opposition to the closure, now backed Fortis's bid.

Fortis was represented by Hilltop Public Solutions, a major political and business consulting firm that has deep ties to both de Blasio's campaign and his administration. It is run by Nicholas Baldick, a top de Blasio campaign advisor. Bill Hyers, de Blasio's campaign manager, and Rebecca Katz, another advisor, worked serially at Hilltop, the campaign, and the de Blasio administration in a revolving-door fashion. When Katz left his office to go back to resume her partnership at Hilltop, de Blasio, at her farewell party, compared his administration to the Eagles' song "Hotel California," where "you can check out anytime you want, but you can never leave."

Fortis also employed James Capalino, a high-powered New York City lobbyist who raised significant money for de Blasio and was one of his closest advisors, speaking to the mayor on a near-daily basis throughout his first term. Capalino is a virtually permanent fixture in New York real estate and government, moving seamlessly between politics and the development of major mixed-use and commercial building projects.

Capalino started out working for Ed Koch in 1972 as a congressional aide in Koch's district office and later managed all of Koch's mayoral election campaigns. He was appointed by Koch to serve as the youngest commissioner of general services in New York City history. In between his stints in government and politics, Capalino as real estate executive managed the development of millions of square feet of downtown Brooklyn and the far west side of Manhattan. If there is a Platonic ideal of "Development Man," bestride the nexus of real estate interests and New York City politics, he is incarnated in the person of Jim Capalino.

This sordid episode—in which de Blasio vociferously protested the sale of a beloved Brooklyn hospital, only then to expedite its sale on behalf of insiders and backers the minute he had power—is emblematic of the low standard of ethics in the de Blasio administration. Again and again Bill de Blasio took pay-to-play politics to Tammany levels of corruption, turning City Hall into something more like a pari mutuel window than the cathedral of transparency and good government he promised to run.

Eventually, de Blasio's money machine faced criminal investigation at every imaginable level. The federal prosecutor, the state commission on ethics, the Manhattan district attorney, and even his own commissioner of investigation were inquiring into his many intrigues. Only because the rest of New York's political class is mired just as deeply in the bogs of transactional politics, and because of a dash of luck, have de Blasio's manifold schemes managed to evade the reach of justice.

· · · · · · · · · ·

Bill de Blasio's political fortunes have always been entangled with money and influence, as illustrated by his long involvement with the Working Families Party (WFP). The WFP is a so-called third party with a radical left agenda—resolutely anti-business, anti-charter school, pro-welfare, and pro-taxes. But owing to a quirk in New York State election law, the WFP is able to leverage significant power well beyond what most Americans assume when they think about minor parties. New York allows for "fusion" voting, which permits candidates to accept the nomination of multiple political parties for the same election: the winner aggregates his or her votes from all ballot lines.

Accepting multiple nominations gives politicians the appearance of having broad appeal and the ability to build consensus. Minor parties attract segments of the electorate that are dissatisfied with the two dominant parties and can gain powerful leverage in exchange for their nomination. For example, the Liberal Party of New York was for many years considered the exemplar of a successful third party, especially following the 1969 reelection of Republican mayor John Lindsay, solely on the liberal line. In 1993 the liberals endorsed Rudy Giuliani in his mayoral election, the first time a Republican was elected mayor in 28 years, and his nomination as a fusion candidate was credited with helping push him over the edge in a close contest.

The WFP was formed following Giuliani's 1997 reelection, again as a fusion candidate. Sal Albanese, a reformist Democratic councilman from Brooklyn, had run for the Democratic nomination and wound up running on the Independence Party ballot line, winning a small number of votes. After the election, Albanese found himself frustrated with the machine politics of the Democratic Party, which he thought to be dominated by real estate and business interests. Organized labor felt similarly alienated from the process because the Democratic machine could take labor support for granted.

Albanese allied with Bob Master, an operative of the Communication Workers of America, to form an alternate political party, composed of labor unions and grassroots activist groups, whose purpose, as Albanese explains it, was to "push the Democratic Party [to be] more receptive to working-class issues." The leaders of the Laborers union, the Machinists, the Communications Workers, and the Auto Workers formed the nascent WFP.

Involved in the early days of the WFP's founding were Jon Kest and Valerie Berlin, lead Association of Community Organizations for Reform Now (ACORN) organizers, and

Bertha Lewis, head of ACORN's New York chapter, who became the WFP cochair. ACORN made news in the 1980s by occupying vacant city-owned buildings in East New York and successfully demanding that the city turn the property over to the squatters. ACORN grew in prestige by organizing around tenant concerns and built an effective organizing presence in poor neighborhoods throughout the city. In 2009, ACORN was the target of an exposé in which outreach workers were taped counseling clients how to commit criminal fraud, and the organization was dissolved.

ACORN's actual paid-up membership was never especially significant in itself, but the group trained hundreds of committed, low-paid professional activists in the practice of canvassing, issue-specific campaign fieldwork, and door-to-door fund-raising. This cadre of housing organizers formed the core of the WFP's legendary field operations and became key to its success. The two organizations operated from the same building, along with the Alliance for Quality Education, a teachers union–funded outgrowth of ACORN that focused on fighting charter schools and capturing as much tax revenue as possible for centralized education.

ACORN was a tenants' rights organization dedicated to radical politics and direct action. But that didn't mean it wouldn't lie down with the running dogs of high capitalism, especially if the price was right. When major developer Forest City Ratner wanted to build a complex of 16 massive mixed-use towers and a sports arena in downtown Brooklyn, many locals pushed back. But ACORN was happy to support the project, especially after it received a $1.5 million grant from Forest City, along with nebulous promises to build affordable housing. ACORN activists and WFP politicians jumped to support the enormous development.

This pattern—a shakedown followed by pan rattling to celebrate the dodgy deal—encapsulates how real estate moguls pay off community advocacy groups and their elected Progressive activist brothers-in-struggle to provide a woke front for mammoth urban renewal projects. Any residual community opposition can always be silenced with sneers of racist NIMBYism.

Bill de Blasio was involved with the WFP from its earliest days, so much so that, as one prominent Democratic insider told the *New York Post*, "Without exaggeration, ACORN's long-range plan since 2001 was to elect de Blasio mayor. De Blasio was a big ACORN project." In 1997, de Blasio joined the staff of city council speaker Peter Vallone, in preparation for Vallone's gubernatorial run the following year. The WFP backed Vallone in his unsuccessful run and thus managed to win the 50,000 votes on its line necessary for automatic four-year ballot status; de Blasio's role as a go-between for Vallone and the WFP executive board helped establish the party's status as a force in New York politics.

Following de Blasio's election to the council in 2001, the WFP backed him for the speakership. Their collaboration continued through his 2005 reelection and in 2006 when he again sought to become speaker. That same year, de Blasio was paid $33,000 by the Progressive America Foundation to perform obscure lobbying services; the Progressive America Foundation operated from the offices of the WFP. This wasn't the first time de Blasio as an elected official raised eyebrows for moonlighting as a political operative: in 2004, while serving as the cochair of the John Edwards presidential campaign in New York, he also held a paid position with the campaign.

In 2009, de Blasio made his first run for citywide office, with the full backing of the WFP, which ran his campaign for public advocate. It was at this point that de Blasio became entangled with one of the most bizarre, convoluted machinations in New York City's political history. The WFP, in preparation for the 2009 election cycle, and following the briefly successful effort to win the state senate for the Democrats in 2008, spun off its renowned field and electoral operations into a subsidiary, Data and Field Services, which could hire itself out on a for-profit basis to WFP-backed campaigns.

But the real purpose of the scheme seems to have been the reallocation of resources and personnel among the WFP's candidates and to enable coordination between campaigns—all of which is illegal, according to New York City's campaign finance laws. With an extraordinarily expensive system of public financing of elections—currently matching donations at a rate of eight to one—New York imposes strict rules regarding how money is raised and how it is spent. Because so many taxpayer dollars are involved, every penny must be tracked. Coordination between campaigns must be strictly accounted for, and consultants, who take in millions of dollars each cycle, must avoid conflicts of interest—say by working for opposing candidates or issues simultaneously.

2009 was a banner year for the WFP, which brought de Blasio and a slate of insurgent Progressive council members into office, ousting Democratic "regulars." The Queens County Democratic Committee, run by power broker and senior Democratic congressman Joe Crowley, was unable to protect incumbents or promote party favorites; less than a decade later, Crowley would lose his own seat to Alexandria Ocasio-Cortez, an even more radical version of a WFP Progressive. (Ironically, the WFP had become so institutionalized and transactional that it gave its 2018 ballot line to Crowley, the epitome of a mainstream, moderate, machine Democrat.)

The WFP set up a series of interlocking and nested entities to handle fund-raising and campaign expenditures for its candidates. By accepting large contributions from unions and other entities who were already "maxed out" by law to underfunded WFP candidates in tough races, the party was able to subsidize their campaign operations or surreptitiously spend beyond legal limits.

In 2013, when de Blasio ran for mayor, his campaign machine leveraged extensive "independent expenditures" from ad hoc groups that by law were not supposed to coordinate with specific campaigns. For instance, superrich horse lovers Stephen Nislick and Wendy Neu nursed dreams of revenge against de Blasio's rival Christine Quinn because she went back on her promise that she, as council speaker, would ban the popular and touristic horse carriage concession around Central Park. Neu and Nislick, fanatically opposed to this tiny industry, hatched a scheme to pour millions of dollars into a campaign to beat Quinn, ostensibly in favor of anyone else, though in reality they were backing de Blasio, who had vowed to embrace and realize their cause.

Nislick-funded organizations New Yorkers for Clean, Liveable, and Safe Streets (NYCLASS) and New York City Is Not for Sale set up the "Anybody but Quinn" campaign through former ACORN spokesman Scott Levenson's

Advance Group, which loaned office space to former ACORN boss Bertha Lewis. Levenson, Anybody but Quinn, and the United Federation of Teachers eventually wound up being investigated by the FBI for financial improprieties, including funneling payments through a fake consulting group to disguise the fact that the Advance Group was working on competing campaigns.

At the same time that the WFP was expanding its reach and taking over city government, ACORN veterans Jonathan Rosen and Valerie Berlin formed consulting firm BerlinRosen, which was central to the planning and execution of the rise of de Blasio and the Progressive wing of the Democrats to power. BerlinRosen, the Advance Group, and other consulting firms, including Red Horse Strategies, run by leftist staffers of the state senate Democrats, prospered richly under the WFP/de Blasio ascendancy. Together they booked more than $7 million in consulting fees for the 2013 municipal elections alone.

But these outfits don't limit themselves to helping politicians get elected and stay in office: they also serve as consultants to labor unions, real estate development corporations, and issue-based organizations—all seeking access to the halls of power. None of these firms are obligated to disclose who their clients are or the fees they collect because they don't call themselves "lobbyists."

· · · · · · · · · ·

Upon taking office, instead of dismantling his formidable campaign operation or putting it on the back burner as elected officials normally do, Bill de Blasio converted it into a nonprofit political fund-raising organization. Called the Campaign for One New York (CONY), this entity was ostensibly charged with promoting the mayor's Progressive agenda—eliminating income inequality, gentrification, and police brutality and establishing universal prekindergarten. Managed by his campaign finance director Ross Offinger, CONY was supposedly a stand-alone, nonpartisan issues-advocacy group.

De Blasio claimed that he needed to establish an organization because his office lacked the resources to wage an advertising and media war of ideas against well-heeled opponents who were fighting to destroy the revolutionary energy of his mayoralty. De Blasio explained

> So, we come along and say here's our core agenda, it revolves around fighting income inequality, things like creating full-day, pre-K for all, and a very ambitious affordable housing program for half-a-million people. We're going to put together the resources to achieve those goals—those are going to be fights. They were fights—you got to see it with your own eyes. . . . We were trying to break a status quo that was very well entrenched.

Yet neither of these policy efforts was ever actually opposed by "entrenched" interests. The mayor's call for universal pre-K was supported by nearly everyone. What generated opposition was de Blasio's insistence that the program be funded by a special tax on high incomes, a proposal that state leaders rejected as politically unfeasible. In the end, Democratic New York governor Andrew Cuomo found funding for the program in the state budget, and business leaders and Progressives alike celebrated its launch.

As for affordable housing, de Blasio's plan to reshape New York City through rezoning did receive pushback—but not from the entrenched real estate industry or the billionaires behind it. In fact, John Banks, president of the Real Estate Board of New York, an industry group comprising the city's major developers, wrote in support of mandatory inclusionary housing, calling it "crucial" and "a sensible tool in the belt of the mayor to promote the construction of new affordable housing."

De Blasio always got along well with the real estate industry. The opposition to his plan came, ironically, from community groups and affordable-housing advocates, who argued that the mayor was destroying neighborhoods, promoting gentrification, and not pushing wealthy developers hard enough to build "deeply affordable" units for very poor or homeless people.

Stripped of its populist facade, CONY was simply a funnel for New York City's donor class to pour millions of dollars into team de Blasio's open pockets. Virtually all the money that went into CONY came from big labor, developers who needed city approval for their projects, or wealthy advocates for pet causes. And almost all the money that flowed out of CONY—millions of dollars—went to consulting firms run by individuals with deep, long, and personal ties to Bill de Blasio and to the same groups that had donated the money in the first place.

For instance, the American Federation of Teachers gave CONY hundreds of thousands of dollars. One of de Blasio's first actions as mayor was to give the New York City teachers' union a huge contract, including retroactive raises, worth $5 billion. Under Bloomberg's administration, negotiations between the union and the city stalled, which meant that the teachers' existing contract was carried over, including automatic seniority-based pay increases. However, the teachers did not receive any *additional* raises for the final few years of Bloomberg's mayoralty.

De Blasio quickly remedied this alleged penalty by giving the teachers two 4 percent raises, backdated to 2009 and 2010, plus an additional 10 percent raise by 2018. This multibillion-dollar payout was so enormous that it had to be spread out through 2020, meaning that while the city was undergoing its severe COVID-related fiscal contraction, it was making payouts to teachers for work they had done more than a decade earlier.

1199SEIU, the largest union local in the country, also gave generously to CONY. UNITE HERE, the large hospitality industry union, formerly run by de Blasio's cousin John Wilhelm, also gave significant money to CONY.

A number of real estate developers with business before the city received calls from de Blasio or his fund-raiser and advisor, über-lobbyist James Capalino, urging them to contribute to CONY; they obliged. Horse lovers Wendy Neu and Stephen Nislick contributed well over $100,000 to CONY as a reminder to de Blasio that he had promised "on day one" of his administration to ban horse carriage rides in Central Park.

Of the close to $4 million that CONY took in, roughly half flowed to BerlinRosen, Hilltop, and AKPD Message and

Media, all run by close de Blasio allies and confidantes. In 2016, amid a federal investigation into CONY and a host of other scandals, de Blasio posed a novel legal maneuver to shield his communications with these advisors, insisting that as "agents of the city" their discussions with him were privileged and not subject to disclosure. This designation— which had no basis in law or custom and was eventually rejected by the courts—was applied to five men.

Jonathan Rosen, with whom de Blasio reportedly talked for hours per day in his first term, though he insisted only about personal matters, never politics or business, was the primary agent. Rosen represented multiple major real estate developers who donated to the mayor's election campaign and to CONY and was permitted by de Blasio to participate in high-level policy meetings regarding his signature city-wide rezoning plan.

Bill Hyers (de Blasio's 2013 campaign manager) and Nicholas Baldick, both of Hilltop, booked more than a quarter-million dollars from CONY. Baldick previously founded the Alliance for a New America—former North Carolina senator John Edwards' independent campaign finance vehicle for his 2008 presidential campaign. The Alliance was later implicated in campaign finance fraud scandals.

John Del Cecato, another "agent of the city," is a founding partner of consulting powerhouse AKPD Message and Media. Del Cecato had at least 60 meetings with de Blasio in the first 18 months of the mayor's administration. AKPD billed CONY more than $1.1 million for its communications work.

The fifth agent was de Blasio's best friend, Patrick Gaspard, the US ambassador to South Africa under Obama and until the end of 2020 the president of the Open Society Foundations, the $20 billion grant-making network funded by George Soros. In addition to donating to CONY, Open Society–linked foundations have been tied to funding Black Lives Matter protests, promotion of anti-Israel agitation on college campuses, and efforts to destabilize nationalist governments in Eastern Europe, among other hard left causes.

The "agents of the city" scheme was cooked up, incidentally, by Maya Wiley, de Blasio's chief counsel. Wiley, who announced her candidacy to succeed de Blasio as mayor in October 2020, is the daughter of George Wiley, one of the founders of the radical National Welfare Rights Organization (NWRO). The NWRO, which worked with the Black Panthers and the Young Lords, organized welfare recipients to occupy offices, stage demonstrations, and demand unrestricted direct cash payments to the poor—an early version of a guaranteed national income—and was the direct predecessor organization to ACORN. Maya Wiley also has a long history of work with the Open Society Foundations, in late 1990s' South Africa with its Criminal Justice Initiative, and later with the Soros-funded Center for Social Inclusion, whose "mission is to catalyze community, government, and other institutions to dismantle structural racial inequity."

A chief engineer in the rise of Bill de Blasio was Emma Wolfe, de Blasio's closest political strategist throughout his career. Wolfe started out as an ACORN organizer, worked for 1199 SEIU and the WFP as a political director, and then joined de Blasio's team as chief of staff of the public advocate's office. She has been a constant presence in his career, ascending to the role of chief of staff and deputy mayor for administration. One of the most powerful and savvy people in city government, Wolfe maintains a low public profile. But her girlfriend, political operative Stephanie Yazgi, was a director of CONY and then given a $150,000 job as "campaign director" in the Mayor's Office of Immigrant Affairs, "overseeing the mayor's national organizing efforts on immigration, specifically the Cities for Action on Immigration coalition."

At the same time that he was allowing consultants to use City Hall as a watering hole for their clients and his donors, effectively allowing them to oversee and guide the creation of legislation that would govern their industry, and creating no-show patronage jobs for hundreds of well-connected insiders throughout city government, Bill de Blasio spoke out fiercely and vigorously against the undemocratic, corrosive, and outsized influence that consultants have on the political process. "Despite their growing role in our elections, we know very little about this new breed of social welfare groups," public advocate de Blasio proclaimed at a public hearing in 2013. "They often hide behind ambiguous names. . . . These sham nonprofits are not only a threat to our democracy but also to the integrity of our nonprofit sector." He continued

> It is past time to shine a public spotlight on political committees that masquerade as tax-exempt nonprofits. We know that the vast majority of social welfare groups, such as

volunteer fire departments, Rotary clubs, veterans' organizations, and community groups provide great benefit to our society. These sham nonprofits do not.

But CONY was a "sham nonprofit" par excellence. All it did was move money through de Blasio's office into the hands of his friends, while he skimmed some off the top to fund his efforts to build a national profile as a Progressive kingmaker.

De Blasio's shenanigans intensified as he settled into his job; CONY was just a prelude to a series of pay-to-play scandals that turned City Hall inside out and which in a healthy system would have led to the arrest of the mayor and his inner circle for blatantly corrupt activity.

In an attempt to swing the state senate permanently to the Democrats—the dream of the Progressive left for decades— in 2014 de Blasio embarked on a scheme to funnel contributions to weaker candidates statewide. New York State's campaign finance laws are looser than the city's, but there are still rules about how much an individual can contribute to a candidate. The limits are much higher, however, regarding contributions to a county party organization. De Blasio's campaign treasurer Ross Offinger—also the treasurer of CONY—worked this loophole, instructing donors to contribute large sums to the Democratic Party committees of small upstate counties, apparently "earmarking" them to particular candidates, which is a felony. De Blasio supposedly would leave the room right before these requests were made and return immediately after. So tiny party committees in Putnam or Ulster counties, which would occasionally receive $500 donations, were suddenly flooded with hundreds of thousands of dollars from major downstate developers and labor unions.

Piling another scoop of iniquity atop this sundae of venality, the senate campaigns receiving these funds were reportedly ordered to spend the money with the consulting firms in de Blasio's orbit, thus closing the circle. Major players from the mayor's staff, labor unions, and political consulting firms were documented in subpoenaed emails as coordinating in this effort.

In 2016, news emerged that the city had lifted a deed restriction on a former nursing home on Rivington Street, on the trendy Lower East Side. The building's deed specified that it could only be used for purposes related to healthcare; lifting this restriction enabled the owner to sell the building to a luxury real estate developer for many times more than it was otherwise worth. Jim Capalino, the city's top-grossing lobbyist and a chief fund-raiser and advisor to Bill de Blasio, represented both the original owner of the nursing home and its ultimate purchaser.

Capalino denied having any involvement in the deal, though his fingerprints were all over it. A memo offering justifications for changing the deed, circulated by the Department of City Administrative Services, was later found to have been composed by someone at Capalino's firm. Politico reported that

> Capalino's stable of lobbyists were so entrenched in the minutiae of de Blasio's first term, they formed an unofficial, additional layer of government—sometimes instructing

staffers how to do their jobs—all while advancing the interests of their paying clients.

In an even more surreal case, Harendra Singh, a Queens restaurateur, was a key witness in the 2018 federal corruption trial of Ed Mangano, the Nassau county executive. In the course of his testimony, it emerged that Singh had already pled guilty, in 2016, to charges that he had bribed Mayor de Blasio to get favorable lease-renewal terms on a restaurant he ran on city-owned land. According to Singh, de Blasio asked him to raise substantial amounts of money to help other politicians. When Singh remarked that he would have to pay donors back for their contributions, the mayor told him, "I don't want to know. Just do whatever you got to do."

The mayor denied all of this, claiming that "nothing that he describes as having happened, happened—period," though it is stipulated and accepted that de Blasio and Singh met several times, that Singh gave ample money to de Blasio and his assorted campaigns, and that Singh did receive special treatment from City Hall. "This guy, to save his own skin, struck a plea deal with the federal prosecutors," insisted de Blasio. "He agreed to certain charges for his own self-preservation."

Similarly, Jona Rechnitz, a Brooklyn businessman who donated heavily to de Blasio and could get him on the phone whenever he wanted, wound up pleading guilty to federal charges of bribing the mayor. "I worked with straw donors," he told the court, explaining how he would ask people to give money to political campaigns on behalf of the mayor, with the understanding that Rechnitz would pay them back. When he explained to Ross Offinger at one point that he would solicit money from people he worked with, on the basis of future repayment, Rechnitz testified, Offinger got "red in the face" and said, "I can't hear that. Just give me the checks."

As with Singh, de Blasio denied ever soliciting money from Rechnitz on a quid pro quo basis and called him "a very bad person," though of course he couldn't deny knowing the men, meeting them frequently, speaking with them on the phone, and taking their money. Nor could he deny that Singh and Rechnitz were able to get things done through their association with the mayor's office. But that didn't stop the mayor from blustering about how carefully his team vetted everything they did and proclaiming self-righteously that "we can show you how we very scrupulously followed the law and followed the ethical guidance." He also averred that

> the law is law—what we did—everything was very carefully and scrupulously checked for consistency with city, state, and federal law for absolute consistency with any other standards that had to be held. We didn't do any of this lightly.

The bizarre thing about these cases is that one man can go to federal prison for admitting to bribing an official, while the official in question can be reelected to office, take trips to Florida to watch the Red Sox prepare for Opening Day, and then launch a run for president—almost like there are different sets of laws that apply to politicians versus everyone else. You would think that bribery is a dance that requires two participants. But the one-sided tango is reminiscent of an old saying about a plate of ham and eggs: the chicken is involved, but the pig is committed.

With all his talk about scruples and scrupulousness, it is hard to understand how the mayor wound up bogged down in a multiyear ethics investigation involving multiple jurisdictions and at least half a dozen lines of inquiry. After all, if he was so painstaking about minutely charting the limits of legality and so intensely conscientious about staying within those lines, isn't it bizarre—almost like something out of Franz Kafka—that de Blasio somehow fell under so much prosecutorial scrutiny?

The mayor spoke to this seeming injustice, musing, "I'm really concerned about a double standard here where we do everything to the letter of the law . . . meanwhile, a lot of people are doing a lot worse and not getting much examination." He used the phrase "letter of the law" repeatedly, emphasizing how closely he and his team hewed to every jot and tittle of the code.

The curious thing about scrupulously following the "letter of the law" is that it sounds like an excuse for bad behavior. When someone gets away with something on a "technicality," it usually means that under the "letter of the law" they couldn't be convicted. Bragging about having "scrupulously" observed the letter of the law sounds a bit like saying under oath, "I did not have sexual relations with that woman."

Even at the low point of the mayor's time in office, in the spring of 2020, when COVID-19 deaths were rising rapidly and there were legitimate fears that hospitals would be overrun by patients gasping for breath, de Blasio made time for donors. After insisting that New York would go it alone and produce its own supply of ventilators and protective equipment, the city gave a $91 million contract to Digital Gadgets, LLC, based in New Jersey.

Digital Gadgets had no experience in manufacturing breathing apparatus; in fact, the company appears mostly to be an importer and distributor of Chinese-made hoverboards, headsets, and small electronics for QVC. But its owner, Charlie Tebele, along with family members, did contribute $44,000 to the mayor's 2020 presidential run and to his Fairness PAC, established as an ostensible counterweight to the "dark money" that de Blasio claims dominates national politics.

When de Blasio's announced his run for president in 2019, it sounded like the ultimate folly. His popularity in New York City was anemic. His national stature was Lilliputian, despite years of travel and a concerted effort to raise his profile. Yet it's a mistake to think that de Blasio's presidential bid was only a vainglorious ego trip. As the middleman in a machine that runs on money, it was vital for him to maintain a vehicle for fund-raising, or he would deprive the machine of the pump that keeps the cash flowing.

De Blasio ran City Hall like a financial pass-through entity to facilitate his donors' business and keep his high-placed consultant friends happy. When he announced his bid, he had about two good years left in office to generate donations, but he couldn't accept contributions if he had nowhere to put them: you can't be a bagman with no bag. It's illegal for his donors to give him money personally, so he needed a plausible excuse to continue to accept contributions.

. . . .

Many New York State elected officials, and their bribers and other enablers in corruption, have gone to prison in the last 10 years, almost all through the federal court system. It's not that New York lacks state or local oversight of corruption; in fact, New York has some of the nation's strongest anti-corruption laws and multiple cross-jurisdictional agencies that can address political malfeasance of any sort.

County district attorneys, responsible for prosecuting violations of state and local law, are the primary legal players in public corruption cases. New York State's attorney general is technically barred from prosecuting bribes and violations of election law, though former attorney general Cuomo radically expanded the power of that office when he investigated former governor Eliot Spitzer's use of state police to spy on his political enemies. The state's former attorney general, Eric Schneiderman—who was forced to resign in disgrace when it emerged that he has a penchant for beating up his sex partners—established the Public Integrity Bureau to handle "complex investigations into government corruption, fraud and abuse of authority."

The Joint Commission on Public Ethics (JCOPE), a state-level authority, has jurisdiction over public employees and elected officials. In New York City, the Campaign Finance Board (CFB) investigates compliance with Gotham's expansive laws in this area, the city council has wide (and untapped) subpoena power, and the Department of Investigation has broad oversight over every aspect of municipal government, including the power to investigate people or entities that receive benefits from or do business with the city.

All these overlapping state and local entities should be elbowing one another out of the way to bring malefactors to judgment, but none appears committed to the task. Dozens of elected officials have gone to prison since 2000, virtually all convicted by the US Department of Justice. Why must New Yorkers rely on the federal government to police local corruption?

Much of the problem—unsurprisingly—lies in New York's interlinked networks of donors, party bosses, unions, and consultants, who choose candidates, fund them, and essentially control them once they're in office. Four of the city's five district attorneys and Attorney General Letitia James all come from the same pool of Progressive Democratic Party politics and are all essentially allies of the mayor—or at least it's understood that they all play on the same team. JCOPE is dominated by the governor, and he and the legislature appoint toothless watchdogs to oversee their own ethics violations. The mayor, meanwhile, controls the CFB, which ignores his million-dollar excesses while scrutinizing every penny spent by his opponents.

Power adores a vacuum. While New York's assorted enforcement personnel circle around one another, it's no surprise that unelected federal prosecutors, who make their names by hunting the biggest heads, have rushed in. So why isn't de Blasio in a federal prison now?

Prosecutor Preet Bharara of the Southern District of New York, the federal prosecutor who seemed closest to dropping the hammer on de Blasio, was fired by Donald Trump shortly after his inauguration. The reasons for this were never made clear, but suspicions abound that de Blasio and Trump—despite their mutual antipathy—nonetheless had high-placed mutual friends in the rarefied spheres of Manhattan billionaire real estate developers, who may have had a quiet word with the president that certain of their dealings involving the mayor would be better off undisclosed.

The same day that Bharara's successor as federal prosecutor announced that he would drop the investigation into de Blasio's fund-raising skullduggery, Cy Vance, the Manhattan district attorney, announced that his office would also end its investigations into de Blasio and his schemes to flip the state senate. But Vance was also a major client of Mark Guma Communications, which was subpoenaed by state ethics investigators in regard to its role as a go-between in de Blasio's state senate financing scandal. Vance paid Mark Guma Communications more than $1.3 million in consulting fees from 2009 to 2013.

Cy Vance, it's worth noting, is also the prosecutor who quashed allegations that Harvey Weinstein had sexually assaulted actress Ambra Battilana; Vance, it emerged, had received $55,000 in campaign contributions from Weinstein's lawyer, Democrat powerbroker David Boies. According to *New York Magazine*, Battilana's credibility was immediately attacked by Vance's investigators, who appeared to be more concerned with protecting Weinstein than with determining the truth of the allegations. NYPD sex crime detectives were so leery about continuing to cooperate with Vance's office that they hid Battilana, under an assumed name, in a hotel for five days in April 2015.

It's not that Letitia James, Andrew Cuomo, Bill de Blasio, Cy Vance, and all the other elected officials in New York are buddies. But they are, in a sense, coworkers employed by the same set of bosses. Big real estate and big labor pay heavy-hitter consultants to keep the juice flowing. The consultants help pick the candidates for office, raise money for them, spend the money, and tell the candidates whose backs to rub and when. So it's not surprising that they would all pass the buck on investigating each other or that corruption would be allowed to fester. You can't expect a pimple to pop itself.

6

Nowhere to Go:
New York and
the Homeless

A T THE END OF 2013, following Bill de Blasio's victory in the mayoral election, the *New York Times* ran a major five-part feature called "Invisible Child," focused almost entirely on the experiences of an 11-year-old girl named Dasani Coates. The child lived in a homeless shelter with her mother, seven siblings, and her mother's boyfriend, who was father to several of the other children. Dasani served as a primary caregiver to her younger brothers and sisters, as her parents were lost in their dysfunctional lives, incapable of holding down jobs or staying sober.

The heartbreaking story was read widely across New York and the nation, and its implicit message was that the outgoing Bloomberg administration after 12 years had apparently failed to solve the root social causes that led to the Coates family's homelessness. The incoming Progressive ascendency embraced this narrative. Letitia James walked hand-in-hand with young Dasani to her inauguration as public advocate and announced that the girl was her "new BFF." James later said that she played a key role in bringing the story to the attention of the *New York Times*, a claim that turned out to be entirely false. For his part, one of Mayor de Blasio's first major actions on homelessness was to move hundreds of children and their families out of the Auburn Family Shelter in Brooklyn, where Dasani lived in well-documented squalor.

Homelessness is endemic in New York City, which has more homeless people—approximately 60,000—than anywhere else in the nation. The impression people have of the demographic composition of the homeless is skewed, however, because the less visible segment of the homeless population, who live in city-sponsored shelters, is in fact much more numerous than the homeless people we are accustomed to seeing on the streets of Manhattan, who define the public sense of what constitutes homelessness. Many cities—owing to fairer climates—have much more street homelessness than New York. But no other place in the country has so many homeless families or spends so much on them.

New York is unique because, following a series of lawsuits in the 1970s and 1980s, the state consented judicially to establish a legal "right to shelter." Originally applied only to homeless men in the 1981 Callahan consent decree, the right was expanded, separately, to homeless women in 1983 and families in 1986. The Callahan decree described the absolute obligation of New York City to provide people in need of shelter with a bed and bedding, laundry services, showers, secure storage, and food. Originally, the plaintiffs in the Callahan case demanded that the city provide 750 emergency beds to ease overcrowding in the existing system, which sheltered about 2,500 men and women in 1981, at an annual cost of about $30 million, adjusted for inflation.

Almost 40 years later, New York City provides shelter for almost 60,000 people every night and spends about 100 times as much money—in constant dollars—on homeless services as it did 40 years ago. About one-quarter of these homeless people (roughly 14,000) are single adult men; another 5,000 are single adult women. Families with children comprise the largest segment of the sheltered population, including 18,000 children and their parents—frequently single mothers. Thousands of others are unsheltered and sleep on the streets, in the subways, in parks, or wherever else they can find a spot. This latter population is highly visible, includes many untreated seriously mentally ill people, and describes who most people think of when they think of the "homeless."

The visibility of street homelessness, for better or worse, is a leading indicator of how New Yorkers gauge "quality of life." The extent to which the city permits occupation of its public spaces by people who have nothing to do and nowhere to go—and allows those spaces to become dominated and defined by antisocial behavior or the persistent occupation by derelicts—is a measure of the disintegration of civic life. New York, especially Manhattan, is extremely dense, and its habitability is determined largely by the way in which its citizens peaceably share precious public space.

When parks and plazas have a flow of varied activity—sunbathers, flaneurs, loungers, office workers eating lunch, musicians, joggers, children—they are warm, harmonious places representing the bounty and exuberance of urban life. And there is room within this symphony of varied human existence for the least fortunate among us, who also need somewhere to go. But when public places become magnets for the homeless, prosocial activity is driven out, and these spots become zones of dysfunction, where addicts and drug dealers congregate, quarrels are aired and disputed, and people feel free to expose their lower nature generally. Law-abiding residents in search of respite from the business of their day are frightened off, which encourages the further spiraling down and degradation of public areas.

Over the last few years, for example, the lower concourse of Grand Central Terminal, which includes a mall-style food court, has become packed with homeless people, some sleeping upright on benches, some parked at tables with bags and belongings, some wandering around or standing stock still in the middle of the floor.

Grand Central was built as a temple to the gods of railroad travel. After World War II and the end of the golden age of the train, the station entered a long decline that paralleled the fortunes of New York City generally. In the 1970s and 1980s, as public spaces throughout the city became increasingly disorderly and dangerous, Grand Central deteriorated into squalor, with derelicts inhabiting the once-grand waiting room. In 1973, Grand Central's operators announced that the terminal would begin closing for several hours overnight; they blamed declining passenger service, but news reports also cited "problems with prostitutes, vagrants, derelicts and alcoholics."

New York's infamous degeneration throughout the 1980s in many ways centered on Midtown Manhattan, at the heart of which stands Grand Central Station. Times Square, seedy for decades, became the focus of the city's sex and drug trades. Bryant Park—nine acres of green space behind the main branch of the New York Public Library—became a notorious site for drug sales, prostitution, and muggings. Aggressive panhandlers and street hustlers accosted pedestrians, turning midtown into a no-go zone for tourists and families. Mobil Oil abandoned its corporate headquarters on East 42nd Street. The company made a brief video of conditions around its offices, showing filthy streets, derelicts, and decayed infrastructure, contrasting these images with others showing the leafy, clean, suburban office park to which it was relocating. Clearly, New York City had to do something to revive its core.

The creation of business improvement districts (BIDs), with the power to levy taxes on local businesses to supplement municipal services like sanitation, security, and public amenities became key to midtown's revitalization. Starting around 1980, businesses formed the Bryant Park Corporation, which organized extra park maintenance, security, and public programming to attract office workers to eat lunch there during the day. The Bryant Park Corporation achieved official BID status in 1986, around the same time that businesses a few blocks east were forming the Grand Central Partnership to address QoL problems that had turned the terminal into a waystation for homeless people. As the then-largest BID in New York City—covering 70 blocks of prime midtown real estate—the Grand Central Partnership rebuilt street furniture, hired state-certified security officers, provided supplementary maintenance and sanitation, and significantly, contracted with nonprofit social-services providers to reach out to homeless people and connect them to shelter.

Efforts to improve the area through the 1990s paralleled a concerted effort on the part of city leadership to reverse New York City's deterioration. The NYPD broadly implemented broken windows policing, driving down crime and making public spaces safe again by containing minor disorder before it spread and intensified. Crime, which reached a peak in 1990 and fell rapidly thereafter. Police deterred aggressive panhandlers and scam artists and pursued arrests for low-level violations.

In midtown, major rehabilitation projects overhauled key destinations throughout the 1990s: Bryant Park was redesigned and rebuilt, Grand Central Terminal was thoroughly renovated, and Times Square was "Disneyfied" through the closure of its notorious sex shops and pornographic theaters. Tourism rose as crime and disorder declined, and major companies, instead of fleeing New York, recommitted to the city's future. Grand Central became an important fixture on tourists' "must-see" lists, with upscale shopping and gourmet dining options.

But under de Blasio and the Progressive ascendency, New York has seen a turn toward seediness and decay. When dozens of illegal immigrants began dressing in knockoff cartoon character costumes, harassing Times Square tourists for money, the mayor floundered for a solution; haplessly, the city established zones where these "performers" could legally continue to bother pedestrians. When drug dealers took over the northwest corner of Washington Square Park, openly selling crack cocaine, meth, and marijuana, the police ran slow patrols through the area, not arresting anyone, but creating short intervals of suppressed sales; eventually, the dealers took over the entire western half of the park.

Junkies nodding out on the streets and sidewalks of Manhattan became a common sight; it was no longer unusual to see addicts in the daytime determinedly probing their arms or legs with a needle to find a usable vein. Clearly disturbed people wearing filthy clothes settled upon a block or corner and remained there for months, muttering or screaming. Construction scaffolds, which sometimes stay up for years, become convenient stretches of sidewalk for the homeless to establish semipermanent campsites. The Department of Homeless Services (DHS) performed theoretical "outreach" to these "clients," proffering services. "Helping someone off the streets can take hundreds of contacts by HOME-STAT outreach teams," DHS explains. "With persistence and compassion, outreach teams engaged homeless New Yorkers 24/7, offering services, support, and safe housing."

But what, really, is the distinction between compassion and stark indifference when the result—sick people lying in their own filth—is the same?

When the pandemic hit in March 2020, subway ridership dropped by 90 percent as commuter traffic seized up almost completely. The trains, which had gradually become a kind of rolling annex for the homeless/mental illness complex over de Blasio's second term, entered total dysfunctionality. Mentally ill homeless people took up permanent residence on the trains, in some cases surrounding themselves with absurd heaps of garbage. Cars stank.

In a gesture of utter defeat, Mayor de Blasio and Governor Cuomo announced at the end of April 2020 that the subway system's overnight service—the very symbol of New York City's brash 24-hour open-for-business attitude—would end, at least temporarily. Ostensibly, the goal of the late-night shutdown was to perform deep cleaning of the cars to rid them of the presence of the coronavirus, but the real reason was to force homeless people off the trains: as long as the system was open, there was no effective means of compelling them to disembark. What a disaster that after so many decades, New York was brought low by its mayor's inability to manage the takeover of the subway system by people who cart all their possessions with them in plastic bags.

An hour into his 2020 State of the City speech—titled "Save Our City"—Mayor de Blasio made a bold announcement: "I want to be clear, this is way out on a limb, but it's what we have to do. We have to end homelessness as we know it in New York City." Coming six years after he had taken office, de Blasio's statement was more than a bit tardy. And it also understated the massive efforts he had already made toward ending homelessness, to little effect. De Blasio did in fact have a clear track record on homelessness; it was just so dismal—so tainted by waste and scandal—that it's no surprise he tried to give himself a clean slate so late in the game.

Most of the city's homeless people live in shelters, including a variety of types of lodging. Many single adults sleep in barracks-style accommodations, with bunk beds in large rooms sleeping dozens of men. Others share smaller rooms, sometimes in hotels. Most homeless families live in apartment-style dwellings, sometimes leased from private owners, sometimes owned directly by the city.

When de Blasio became mayor, promising to address New York's yawning gaps of inequality, the city spent approximately $1.5 billion on homeless services, including $900 million for shelters. Six years later, the figures had more than doubled to a total budget of $3.2 billion, including $1.9 billion for shelters. The number of people in the shelters rose from 51,000 at the time of de Blasio's inauguration in 2014 to more than 60,000 when he started his second term four years later. In a gesture of unblinking, nearly Soviet arrogance, the mayor declared this 20 percent rise in homelessness an unalloyed success: his interventions, he claimed, prevented the sheltered population from hitting 70,000, a projection that his statisticians retroactively predicted.

So where did all that money go? A steadily increasing amount of the city's homeless budget goes to service providers—the groups that run shelters and intake centers, conduct outreach, and offer specialized treatment to people on the street. But given the enormous demand for shelter, numerous regulations on services, and difficulties dealing with the city, it's hard to find top-quality, scrupulously ethical providers. With more than a billion dollars a year flowing to this sector, the city can't seem to ensure that standards are met, while well-positioned insiders—"nonprofiteers"— soak up public money.

Childrens Community Services (CCS) is a Queens-based homeless services provider that fell under federal criminal investigation for allegations of bilking the city of millions of dollars in fake claims and self-dealing. Board members of the organization appear to own its primary vendors, an illegal practice that lets insiders make money coming and going. CCS received hundreds of millions of dollars in city funding since 2014, shortly after it was founded.

By 2017, CCS was one of New York City's largest contractors, though it provided subpar services from the start. It lost a major contract to provide services to homeless families at Manhattan hotels, and a recent review found that the group was sheltering children in substandard accommodations, receiving its third "poor" inspection rating. Nevertheless, the de Blasio administration continued to shovel millions into CCS's coffers, even as it provided babies with broken cribs and unsafe places to play.

Bronx-based social services powerhouse Acacia Network —which has taken in close to a billion dollars in city funding since 2010—garnered attention after a grisly murder in one of its Upper West Side shelters. This came on the heels of a revelation that Acacia executives had unreported ties to the security firm it hired to monitor its facilities and ensure the safety of the residents; insiders had proprietary ties to other vendors, too. Acacia "cluster sites," which house homeless families, have hundreds of outstanding violations. The politically connected Acacia paid its president, Raul Russi, a staggering $800,000 salary.

In 2019, the de Blasio administration agreed to buy 17 buildings from a notorious slumlord who made a fortune renting space to the city for homeless accommodation; the city wanted to convert the buildings into permanent shelters. The Podolsky family, a father and two sons, pled guilty to dozens of felonies connected to grand larceny and tenant harassment in the 1980s. Their buildings routinely had outstanding violations for vermin and structural deficiencies.

Eyebrows were raised when it emerged that the city had contracted to purchase the Podolskys' buildings for $173 million—at least $30 million more than their appraised value. The Podolskys' attorney was Frank Carone, lawyer for the Kings County Democratic Party; an old de Blasio donor, friend, and advisor; and generally a major player in Brooklyn politics and real estate. Additionally, shortly after de Blasio took office in 2014, he received mortgages on his two Brooklyn properties—his own house and the house of his late mother—for more than a million dollars. The mortgages were made by a bank founded and owned by a third Podolsky brother.

The debate about homelessness in New York City is extraordinarily contentious. Groups advocating on behalf of the homeless occupy the moral high ground and demand massive expansion of services and loosening of rules. These organizations promote "Housing First," the idea that stable, permanent housing must be the precondition for any other positive social progress by homeless individuals. According to the advocates, the official policy regarding homelessness, which seeks to move people into the workforce through job training, drug rehab, or mental health services, is totally backward. Education, job skills, sobriety, and mental wellness will come after the homeless people are relieved of the stress of not having a permanent place to call home.

There's little evidence, however, that giving a dysfunctional, poorly educated person a stable, permanent place to live will radically improve their chances for success. Certainly there are cases of people who, through a series of misfortunes, may find themselves out of a job and an apartment temporarily. Individuals who are down on their luck can use a hand up to lift themselves back into self-sufficiency. But it's generally not the case that a non-drug-addicted, mentally and physically stable person with job skills falls into long-term homelessness.

A young woman who drops out of high school, has multiple children by different fathers, and has no vocational skills will not magically improve her life chances by getting an apartment of her own, though things may be better for her children, admittedly. Nor is it clear that a single adult man who has spent his adulthood in semi-unemployment, perhaps with a substance abuse problem or mental illness, will thrive because he has "stable, permanent" housing. Yet the city counts moving such people out of shelters and into an apartment—the rent and utilities of which are entirely covered by the taxpayer—as an unqualified success.

Mayor de Blasio's emphasis on affordable housing has ostensibly aimed to help move homeless people into housing, though advocates note that even its most optimistic projections wouldn't really help more than a few of the very poorest New Yorkers. The mayor's housing plan has largely been premised on letting developers build beyond zoned limits—taller buildings, for instance—in exchange for including a certain percentage of units that will remain permanently subsidized by the market-rate units. This works

as long as the market remains healthy but will never provide enough units. The subsidies, even when substantial,
are usually geared toward middle-income earners, not very
poor people. The demand from leftist politicians and activists for "100 percent affordable" real estate development—
essentially, an expansion of the city's already failing massive
public housing program, paid for by private developers—is
a fantasy.

The wholesale rezoning of neighborhoods for "thicker"
residential and mixed-use development has also smacked up
against local opposition. While urbanists and advocates decry
so-called NIMBYism—"Not In My Back Yard" resistance to
new building—as reactionary, elitist, and racist, opposition
to rezoning in New York City is just as often led by working-class, multiracial coalitions fearing that they will be priced
out of their neighborhoods by gentrification. The matter is
not helped by the hyperregulation of the local rental market,
which distorts the pricing structure, discourages people from
moving even when it would otherwise make sense for them
to do so, and inhibits investment. As a result, there is just not
enough housing for very poor people in what is, after all, one
of the most expensive cities in the world.

Just as schools Chancellor Richard Carranza, speaking
about the pandemic, blithely announced, "[N]ever waste a
good crisis to transform a system," advocates for the homeless rushed to take advantage of COVID-19 as an opportunity
to advance their agenda of ending the shelter system in favor
of housing for all. The collapse in tourism left thousands of
hotel rooms sitting vacant; the city began to rent those rooms
on behalf of shelter denizens. The fact that the hotel industry

had been a close de Blasio ally didn't hurt; the Hotel Trades Council was the only union that endorsed his presidential bid, and he counted major hotel owners among his donors.

A major controversy erupted in late July 2020 when homeless people were moved into hotels on the Upper West Side of Manhattan, all in the vicinity of Upper Broadway. The Upper West Side is one of the most densely populated neighborhoods in the United States and is known for its history of leftist politics, a cantankerous urban sensibility, and a high proportion of college-educated residents. But the district contains significant public housing projects, supportive housing for the mentally ill, rehabs, and the like; the Upper West Side has always had an open, liberal vibe, celebrated and parodied in many films and TV shows.

When local hotels suddenly became the new residence of hundreds of homeless shelter denizens—many of whom were chemically dependent and mentally ill and included dozens of registered sex offenders—the Upper West Side found itself dealing with a major new challenge. The median strip along Broadway became an open-air, 24-hour drug market. Reports of harassment of local women and girls soared, random street violence spiked, and daylight sex acts and public masturbation shocked the neighborhood. Long-time residents who questioned the instant conversion of their neighborhood into a Skid Row were slammed as white supremacists and vilified by activists, advocates, and even local elected officials. Assembly member Linda Rosenthal evoked the memory of the Holocaust. A community group called "Upper West Side Open Hearts" was formed to offer love and support to the homeless residents; this outreach was then cited as evidence of deep community ties that would preclude moving the homeless people anywhere else.

The question of where homeless shelters should be sited is enormously controversial. The de Blasio administration always viewed hotels as a stopgap measure to address the problem and tried to limit their use in favor of a plan to build 90 new homeless shelters around the city, in every community district. The idea was to return homeless people to their original neighborhoods to connect them with family, schools, and other ties. "We know a lot of people are going to say, wait, we don't want anything like that in our neighborhood," the mayor acknowledged. "Well, guess what? Everyone needs to take on their fair share, but we can make it work better if we work together." To demonstrate his seriousness, one of the first new shelter projects de Blasio announced was on 58th Street in Manhattan, in an old hotel backing on to Billionaire's Row, where super-tall luxury buildings house the most expensive real estate in the city.

The city council also put forward a proposal using similar language, called "Doing Our Fair Share, Getting Our Fair Share," which demanded that every neighborhood in the city take on the "burden" of various municipal unpleasantness, including waste transfer stations, water treatment plants, and homeless shelters. "Low-income communities and communities of color still see far more than their Fair Share of local unwanted land uses," the report said.

At the same time that officials tacitly recognize that homeless shelters are an example of an "unwanted land use," advocates insist that homeless shelters and other forms of "supportive housing" either have no impact on local real estate value or are even a net benefit—virtually an amenity. NYU's Furman Center, basically the Vatican of Progressive housing policy, claims that properties near new supportive housing, which is usually built on cheaper land, show stronger than average growth in value in the five years after completion of the project.

But if that's the case, why would any neighborhood object to having homeless shelters built there? They should all be clamoring for more shelters. Similarly, if opposition to homeless shelters is a sign of racism—as the Upper West Side Open Hearts and their elected friends believe—then what does it mean when nonwhite local officials universally resist the construction of homeless shelters in their districts? Similarly, as expert Stephen Eide notes, advocates insist that homeless people are far more likely to be the victims of violence than its perpetrators. But, he writes, "security inside shelters is a major concern, on which the city spends over $200 million annually—how, then, can security outside shelters be considered a non-issue?"

Certainly it is true that homelessness is a housing issue, roughly speaking. Cities with ample cheap housing, like Detroit or Baltimore, do not have massive homeless problems the way expensive cities like New York, San Francisco, or Los Angeles do. But the problem with trying to solve homelessness in New York by building housing for very poor people is that even in a moment of declining appeal, New York City has tremendous internal demand for living space. The city will never subsidize enough housing for every homeless person to have an apartment to himself or herself.

Establishing a "right to shelter" almost 40 years ago set in place a perverse principle of law that the city still suffers under. New York City is one of the most expensive places to live in the country, yet the city requires itself to provide its most valuable commodity—space—for free in theoretically unlimited quantities.

7

Who's Thriving Now?: New York City as Open-Air Asylum

ONE OCTOBER NIGHT IN 2019, Randy Santos stalked sleeping homeless men in Chinatown, killing four of them brutally with a metal bar. The murders shocked New Yorkers and prompted anguished appeals for compassion. Mayor Bill de Blasio said that he was "horrified by this senseless act of violence against the most vulnerable members of our community." Council member Stephen Levin, who chaired the council's General Welfare Committee for 10 years, tweeted, "our neighbors who are living on the street or in shelters are so vulnerable & need this city's compassion." Local council member Margaret Chin demanded that the city "do more than the bare minimum to help the tens of thousands of New Yorkers in our homeless shelters and on our streets . . . maximizing every resource to create more affordable housing now." Council member Carlina Rivera of the Lower East Side and the Bowery said that the murders show "that we've failed as a city at building deeply affordable housing."

None of the officials mentioned the most salient point about the confessed killer, Randy Santos, who was himself homeless: he was a violent predator and drug addict with a long history of arrests for attacking people and was known to suffer from serious mental illness. The previous November, to cite one of four incidents, Santos attacked a store clerk on 35th Street—a notorious drug corridor that frequently looks like something out of *The Lower Depths*—and bit him on the chest. In November 2017, he attacked an Italian banker riding on the subway with his family, breaking a bone in the victim's face, with no provocation.

The Progressives in charge of the city distort the problem by speaking in general terms about kindness and the need for more resources and housing. However, Santos's rampage was not caused by a housing shortage or lack of concern for the needy but by the city's failure to keep him off the streets. As a violent offender known to be mentally unstable, Santos should have been in jail or at least under psychiatric observation. Progressive policies regarding mental illness and homelessness created the conditions where a known violent offender and drug addict was permitted to roam free.

Mental illness and homelessness are separate policy areas that intersect frequently and are often conflated in media reports and in the public mind, probably because de Blasio's approach to both issues has been such an abysmal failure. The case of Randy Santos represents the utter disaster that has resulted from the Progressive approach to social services.

· · · · · · · · · ·

Serious mental illness is a problem that affects roughly 4 percent of the population. If properly treated, the seriously mentally ill can lead relatively normal lives and are frequently productive members of society.

In December 2015, Mayor de Blasio introduced a major initiative to deal comprehensively with the problem of New Yorkers' mental health, called "ThriveNYC." This initiative, comprising 58 different programs and with an $850 million price tag, was to be run by Chirlane McCray, the mayor's wife. The goal of ThriveNYC, according to de Blasio, was to prevent and treat mental illness through education, awareness, and early intervention.

McCray proposed a vision of treatment of mental illness that is largely based on prevention. ThriveNYC, she explained at the kickoff announcement, "includes a broad array of initiatives designed to promote mental health, prevent mental illness, and make it easier for those who are suffering to access the treatment they need." The program would fight stigma, which "has been found to have a serious negative effect on an individual's sense of hope and self-esteem. The stigma alone can increase the severity of symptoms."

One must note that McCray is a copywriter by trade, with no professional experience or training in mental health. To compensate for this deficiency, the City University of New York Graduate School of Public Health and Health Policy (CUNY SPH) awarded her an honorary Doctor of Science degree at its 2017 inaugural commencement. Linda Sarsour, a local agitator, cofounder of the Women's March, and high school graduate, was the commencement speaker. McCray cites her "Sc.D. (honorary)" degree on official ThriveNYC white papers.

Much of the actual work in addressing mental illness, according to McCray, must be based upon principles of talk therapy and nonprofessional mutual aid. "It's not just about psychiatrists, psychologists, social workers. It's about peer specialists," she explained. The city planned to train 250,000 New Yorkers in "Mental Health First" identification, which would enable people to spot signs of depression, anxiety, and other maladies of the spirit in their family, neighbors, and coworkers—in other words, to credential yentas and busybodies.

ThriveNYC was essentially an orientation toward mental *wellness*—as opposed to the critical problem of serious mental *illness*—inspired by Chirlane McCray's experiences growing up in the 1960s and 1970s in western Massachusetts, attending Wellesley, and joining the black feminist Combahee River Collective. McCray is basically a hippie, and her outlook bears the stamp of the human potential movement combined with the consciousness-raising sessions that defined 1970s feminism. Raising personal and political consciousness was based on talk. McCray describes her involvement with the Combahee River Collective as follows:

We just talked. Which was enough. We talked about current events. We talked about our lives. Because the feeling was at that time—black women's lives were not reflected in the information people received. You know, it was therapeutic. People were so isolated.

Chirlane McCray, who speaks often about her own experiences with anxiety and depression, believes in therapy. It's no stretch to say that, broadly speaking, the point of ThriveNYC was to get all of New York City—especially the "black and brown communities"—into therapy. The emphasis on peer-to-peer counseling and the constant encouragement for New Yorkers to call ThriveNYC's mental health hotline demonstrate her quaint faith that all people really need is a good heart-to-heart.

But ThriveNYC was based upon a host of faulty premises. For instance, there is no such thing as prevention of serious mental illness, because science has not discovered its causes. In this regard, McCray is correct in asserting that the problem can strike anyone of any class or race. Serious mental illness frequently emerges in one's mid-twenties, and there is no evidence that teaching children to talk about feelings, exposure to art and music, or any other social or policy intervention will keep someone from developing it. As the late D. J. Jaffe, a tireless advocate and researcher, wrote, "while early intervention can prevent mental illness from becoming more severe and disabling, doing so requires focusing on those who are actually sick, not those who aren't."

Another crucial premise of ThriveNYC is that stigma about mental illness is a significant barrier to treatment. Breaking down the taint of moral failure regarding therapy or care, then, is highly important. McCray explained

> When someone has a mental illness, we respond too often by pushing those people away and marking them with disgrace. This mark of disgrace, this stigma has been found to have a serious negative effect on an individual's sense of hope and self-esteem. The stigma alone can increase the severity of symptoms.

It's true that some people look down on therapy or psychiatric medication as a sign of moral weakness. Many immigrants from poor countries see depression and anxiety as luxury problems for the idle rich. And eliminating stigma of this sort may be a valuable goal. However, there is no evidence that stigma plays any role in keeping people with serious mental illness from seeking treatment. Schizophrenics eating garbage, screaming in the middle of the street, wearing filthy clothes, or shoving people in front of subway trains while naked are not overburdened by the opinions of their neighbors, nor do they avoid psychiatric treatment out of shame.

But the main problem with ThriveNYC is that its focus is completely wrong. The major mental health issue in New York City from a public policy perspective is not the neuroticism, anxiety disorders, or emotional malaise of otherwise functioning individuals, who are estimated to comprise perhaps 20 percent of the population. The problem is the much smaller and much more stubbornly persistent number of people who suffer from serious mental illnesses such as schizophrenia or bipolar disorder, which when untreated can result in the afflicted causing serious harm to themselves or others.

Prior to the 1970s, society dealt with the seriously mentally ill through the widespread use of large institutions. Built and maintained at enormous public expense, mental hospitals housing thousands of people through the early twentieth century were considered beacons of social progress and an enlightened approach to dealing with a problem that for centuries had relegated desperately ill people to ostracization. By the 1960s, mass institutionalization of the mentally ill came under intense scrutiny as sensational media reports of terrible treatment and neglect came to light.

The anti-psychiatric movement contributed to growing pressure to close these institutions. Trained psychiatrists such as R. D. Laing and Thomas Szasz disputed the treatment of schizophrenia as a disease and even questioned the propriety of thinking about mental illness in medical terms. Philosophers like Michel Foucault and Gilles Deleuze and sociologists like Erving Goffman suggested that mental illness is a modern category that serves a social control function. Radical civil libertarians assert that mental illness diagnoses are just a way to police alternative, yet entirely valid, modes of being.

At the same time, advances in psychopharmacology such as the development of chlorpromazine, a powerful antipsychotic marketed as Thorazine, and the later discovery of antidepressants, made it possible for people suffering from serious mental illness to live independently or semi-independently, outside the walls of psychiatric institutions. Society moved toward the deinstitutionalization of its population of mentally ill people, transitioning, in theory, to community-based settings, including group homes and various supportive housing models.

Deinstitutionalization in reality became transinstitutionalization, as large facilities were shut down and their patients moved to localized accommodations. In some cases, these smaller models have been humane and effective. But in many instances, people who would have been in long-term care facilities wind up living on the street or cycling through jails, prisons, homeless shelters, and short-term hospital stays. The state continues to eliminate the number of beds available in psychiatric hospitals; as a result, New York City's jails are effectively the largest mental institution in the state.

New York City estimates that roughly a quarter million adult New Yorkers suffer annually from serious mental illness; about 90,000 of these people go untreated. Most are not violent, though they may live on the streets, befoul themselves, steal habitually, and threaten or harass people, including family members. The untreated seriously mentally ill are much more likely to commit violence than the population at large. Approximately 10 percent of all homicides and 50 percent of mass killings are committed by the untreated seriously mentally ill; 5 to 10 percent of this population can be expected to commit an act of violence each year, which means that 15 to 30 acts of violence are committed daily in New York City by seriously mentally ill people.

Until recently, calls to the police regarding mentally ill people were called "emotionally disturbed person," or "EDP calls"; under ThriveNYC, that nomenclature was declared offensive, and the term is no longer in use. But in 2018, the NYPD responded to almost 180,000 EDP calls, or about 500 every day, close to double the number of such calls from 2009. More than half of EDP calls result in a trip straight to the emergency room. Everyone agrees that this system is broken and that police—the first responders of last resort— should not be in the business of collecting untreated mentally ill people and taking them to the hospital.

EDP calls can range from the relatively harmless to the horrific. For instance, in August 2017 the police were summoned to Bryant Park in Midtown Manhattan, where Daniel Ventre, a park habitué, had ripped the heads off two pigeons and upended the carcasses into his mouth. "I'm a vampire," he told police. "I love to eat and suck the blood out of pigeons." Ventre routinely got arrested around Bryant Park for stealing, smoking pot, jumping onto the rails of the subway, and harassing park goers.

A more tragic EDP call occurred in October 2016 when an NYPD sergeant shot and killed 66-year-old Deborah Danner, an emotionally disturbed woman who attacked officers first with a pair of scissors and then with a baseball bat. Mayor de Blasio and then police commissioner James O'Neill wasted no time blaming the sergeant for not following correct police protocol for responding to mentally distressed individuals. It may well be the case that the responding officers made serious errors, but the real mistake was the city's Department of Health and Mental Hygiene's neglect of Danner's serious mental illness.

Danner's case—like the majority of such cases—was known to the city. Her sister, with whom she lived, was Danner's legal guardian, and the NYPD had been called to their house many times. Like many seriously mentally ill individuals, Danner had cycled through the city's police/ medical complex and was apparently noncompliant with her medical regimen—that is, she didn't take her antipsychotic medicine as prescribed.

"It's the classic situation: someone is supposed to take meds and they go off their meds," de Blasio said at a press conference. "Because of their illness they choose not to take their meds. Once they don't take their meds it is very hard to get them to engage another kind of treatment." Listening to the mayor, one would think that the paradox he outlined has never been addressed before and is a problem for which there is no good solution. But New York, like almost every state, has a robust set of laws supporting what is generally known as "assisted outpatient therapy" (AOT).

Locally, the statute is known as "Kendra's Law," named after Kendra Webdale, who in 1999 was pushed in front of a subway car and killed by Charles Goldstein, a schizophrenic who had been in and out of the mental hospital many times. His noncompliance with treatment was well known to the authorities and to his case manager. He had actually sought help for his most recent episode and had been turned away.

Kendra's Law covers cases where a noncompliant and seriously mentally ill individual has previously been hospitalized and is judicially and medically judged to pose a danger to himself or herself or others. It has proven effective at keeping the mentally ill out of hospitals and shelters and promoting compliance with doctors' orders. The law provides for a six-month period of supervision, during which the subject must comply with treatment or face possible commitment to a hospital. But this rarely happens, because the threat of institutionalization is usually enough to compel people to follow their doctors' orders.

Kendra's Law is remarkably successful at helping the seriously mentally ill live relatively stable lives. The statistics are stunning: violent or harmful behaviors decreased by 44 percent, hospitalizations declined by 77 percent, drug and alcohol abuse decreased by half. Patients reported high levels of satisfaction with their participation in AOT and the costs of care declined substantially, because outpatient treatment was so much cheaper—in financial and human terms—than incarceration or hospitalization.

Despite AOT's track record of success, New York State sparingly chooses to apply Kendra's Law, even in seemingly obvious cases like Deborah Danner's. Liberal critics of involuntary psychiatric commitment, still shuddering from the 1972 Willowbrook exposé, argue that any hint of coercive intervention is a violation of the civil liberties of the mentally ill. As a result, Kendra's Law remains underutilized.

Meanwhile, the de Blasio administration prefers to focus on mental illness as a public health problem, like venereal disease or typhus. Publicity campaigns advise people on how to identify the signs of depression in themselves or their associates. This epidemiological approach to mental illness is inadequate, however, because untreated schizophrenia or mania is not contagious, nor is it hard to recognize.

Part of the reason for this diffuse focus is that serious mental illness is a stubborn problem that is not easily fixed. It is much easier to develop positive-sounding metrics on mental health peer training sessions, calls to wellness hotlines, and outreach to new mothers than it is to convince noncompliant patients with bipolar disorder to take their medication regularly or to reduce the number of psychotic people routinely being shuttled between the streets, locked hospital wards, and jail.

The effective decriminalization of marijuana has not helped matters, either. Though the pot lobby gets outraged at the suggestion that marijuana is anything less than a miracle drug that can successfully treat a range of diseases from insomnia to lupus, cannabis is proven to have a negative impact on brain development for younger people and can induce psychotic episodes in people predisposed to develop mental illness. It's a funny paradox when advocates of marijuana insist that it's a powerful medicine, but—unlike every other medicine known to science—it has no negative side effects and no dangerous dosage level.

It is probably no coincidence that in addition to four counts of murder and one count of attempted murder, Randy Santos was charged with unlawful possession of marijuana. An enthusiastic pot smoker, Santos displayed a meme on his Facebook page that read, "Que fumes marihuana no te hace mala persona [smoking marijuana doesn't make you a bad person]." Despite its reputation as a drug that keeps people calm and mellow, marijuana use has been linked to the development and amplification of mental illness in young people, and violent, mentally ill criminals invariably report regular use.

As a result of deinstitutionalization and the Progressive laissez-faire attitude regarding untreated mental illness, the police wind up on the front lines of dealing with the tragic results. One way de Blasio has chosen to address this problem has been to tell the NYPD to stop using the phrase "emotionally disturbed person"; when all else fails, changing the name of something unpleasant might attenuate the awfulness of the underlying phenomenon, it is hoped.

But advocates have also promoted the idea that the police are the problem because they unnecessarily "escalate" conflict with mentally ill people. They wish to replace police responders to emergency calls involving mentally ill people with crisis response teams consisting of social workers and peers—"individuals with lived experience of receiving mental health services and trained to provide support to others," in the words of a report from public advocate Jumaane Williams.

Williams is one of the most aggressive promoters of police reform in New York City and has been leading the charge to divert mental illness crises from the 911 emergency system. He cites the tragic 2018 example of Susan Muller, "a woman living with a mental health condition—who was known by the police in her local precinct and for whom there was a 'history of police calls,'" who was fatally shot by the police in Queens when they responded to a 911 call about an intruder. Williams left out many salient details of the case. It turned out that Susan Muller herself had called the police, claiming there was an armed woman in her house. She invited the police to search for the intruder and then lunged at them with a 10-inch knife; after refusing to drop the weapon, she was shot. There was no intruder.

According to the procedure favored by Williams and other advocates for civilianization of mental health emergency response, the 911 dispatcher ought to have recognized that Susan Muller was calling from a home where a woman "with a mental health condition" lived. A social worker or EMT should have been dispatched to the emergency, preferably with a peer counselor. These individuals, unlike the police, would presumably have seen through Muller's claim that an intruder was in the house and engaged with her based on the "lived experience" of the peer counselor and the empathy of the social worker. Muller would have responded to the soothing, therapeutic tones of crisis intervention, put her hidden knife back in the kitchen, and instead agreed to accompany the team to a drop-in wellness center where she could collect herself.

The case of Saheel Vassell of Brooklyn is also cited by Jumaane Williams as an example of unnecessary police escalation of a harmless situation. Three separate people called 911 to report that a man was lunging at people and sticking what appeared to be a gun in their faces. Police responded to the scene and shot Vassell as he aimed at them. As it turned out, what he was holding was not a gun—it was a piece of welding equipment that looked like a gun. According to Williams' report, "Vassell was known by community members and the local precinct to have a mental health condition, but had not previously demonstrated threatening or dangerous behavior." Thus, "in an ideal response system," local officers "who had knowledge of Vassell's diagnosis" would have responded to the situation and told him to stop goofing around, or they would have dispatched social workers who would do so more caringly.

This proposal begs so many questions as to be absurd. None of Williams' suggestion bear any scrutiny. Calls to 911 did not identify Vassell by name, so there would be no way for the police to ascertain whether or not the person in question was known to be a friendly neighborhood kook or a violent maniac. It's also not clear why anyone imagines that unarmed social workers or peer counselors would do an effective job of talking down a mentally ill person in the midst of a violent episode—and who's to say they would relish the mission in the first place? It's well and good for an elected official to say that unarmed social workers ought to be the first responders to the scene of a violent break with reality, but there's not a lot of social workers joining this call.

· · · · · · · · · ·

In 2018, a major scandal broke when it emerged that ThriveNYC was unable to account for hundreds of millions of dollars that had flowed into its dozens of subsidiary programs. This has been interpreted to mean that Chirlane McCray essentially stole close to a billion dollars, but—to be fair—that's not really accurate. Was ThriveNYC money assigned to community-based organizations and nonprofits to provide outreach and training on mental health without proper accountability? Yes. But ThriveNYC was largely just a rebranding exercise that wrapped existing programs in the "Thrive" label. The failure to account for money that was spent under ThriveNYC is at least in part a measure of how poorly defined ThriveNYC was to begin with.

The Mayor's Management Report (MMR) for ThriveNYC offers a set of metrics whose definitions shift from year to year, making it impossible to gauge progress, and which indicate only vague goals to begin with. We are told in the notes to the 2020 MMR

> The indicator "Requests from veterans, family members and caregivers that resulted in a successful connection to care, services or resources (with DVS)" was revised to "Veterans, family members and caregivers who were successfully connected to care, services or resources through VetsThriveNYC (with DVS)" since the data values represent a count of individuals and not requests.

The revised definition of this metric, whose significance is dubious, did allow ThriveNYC to demonstrate that it had exceeded its own targets by close to 300 percent. Despite its notable lack of success in achieving any but the least meaningful goals, ThriveNYC kept plugging along. Bureaucratic inertia combined with a baselined revenue line can animate even the most decrepit mummy of a social program.

In October 2020, after several people were pushed onto the subway tracks by strangers, a reporter asked Mayor de Blasio, "What is ThriveNYC doing to address the mentally ill homeless, especially those underground?" The mayor's pro forma answer is worth quoting in full to appreciate maximally its irrelevance, defeatism, and basic lack of concern.

> Thrive is here to cover the whole range of mental health challenges. And it begins with giving all New Yorkers,

including their loved ones, the ability to reach out via 8-8-8-NYC-WELL, and connect anyone to mental health services. And that might be someone who's having a simpler problem or someone who's had a historic problem making sure we can get them the more intensive support they need. And there's a lot of work with Thrive, working directly with the NYPD to make sure that mental health professionals are available to address more serious problems. So that's—we've seen obviously, a huge uptick in the amount of New Yorkers turning to Thrive across the spectrum. And I want to encourage that. I want to encourage anyone if there's someone in your life with a problem, pick up that phone and call 8-8-8-NYC-WELL, so we can get the help that you need.

Crazy people wandering the streets and subways and pushing people onto train tracks are a major concern; ThriveNYC and the NYC-WELL hotline are possibly useful programs to help mildly depressed people access services. But there is a significant discontinuity between the problem and the solution. The fact that de Blasio approached the issue of handling the city's thousands of untreated seriously mentally ill individuals by giving it to his wife to manage as a vanity project is certainly one of the greatest failures of his administration and one of the major factors leading to the decline of New York City.

8

Equity Over Excellence:
The Failure of the Schools

IN SPRING 2019, A group of New York City high school students staged walkouts from class in protest of the "segregation crisis" afflicting the public school system. According to the student group Teens Take Charge, the practice at many schools of "screening" kids on the basis of test scores, grades, attendance, or other factors amounted to de facto racial segregation. Teens Take Charge, ostensibly a grassroots student-led organization, was in fact organized and funded by major national educational reform groups such as Leadership for Educational Equity, whose chairperson is Michael Bloomberg's daughter Emma.

The obsession with school screening as a major contributing factor to racial and income inequality is not new but has achieved purchase under de Blasio. In December 2020, the mayor announced that the "COVID era" had reinforced his "commitment to fighting disparities and inequality in every part of the life of New York City," starting with the elimination of screened schools. "I like to say very bluntly," he continued, "our mission is to redistribute wealth. A lot of people bristle at that phrase—that is in fact the phrase we need to use."

But what do screened schools really have to do with the redistribution of wealth? Many critics assume that it's a question of funding and that the selective schools receive more money than nonscreened schools, but all New York City schools are funded more or less equitably, on a per-student basis. The real problem is the fact that the admission processes—no matter how objectively designed and race blind—invariably favor whites and Asians to the detriment of blacks and Latinos. After decades of trying to overcome this disparity with a scalpel, the Progressives have finally decided to attack it with a hammer.

· · · · · · · · · ·

With a student body of 1.1 million, 1,800 schools, an annual operating budget approaching $27 billion, and 135,000 full-time employees, New York City's Department of Education is not just the largest single school system in the country; in many ways it is as complex in its physical infrastructure and politics as a major American city. Its teachers' union, the UFT, is among the most powerful municipal unions in the United States, and the system's employees and other "stakeholders," including parents, elected officials, and advocates, are a major political force citywide.

Per pupil, the New York City schools outspend every large school district in the country. New York State itself spends more per student—about $23,000 as of 2019—than any other state. And New York City spends upward of $25,000 per pupil in its public school system, which is more than double the national average.

Given such enormous expenditures and assuming substantial economies of scale, one would expect New York City to be doing a fantastic job educating its children, but this turns out not to be true. The National Assessment of Educational Progress (NAEP) test is generally considered to be the gold standard of measuring how well school districts do, relative to each other, in testing a random sample of fourth and eighth graders every two years. New York City scores below the national average and also underperforms the rest of New York State.

That doesn't necessarily mean everything, of course—New York City has its own challenges, including many kids who live in poverty, are homeless, or are immigrants or the children of immigrants who don't speak English at home, and so on. There is an entire subindustry of education professionals, working for nonprofit organizations or think tanks associated with the teachers' union, and journalists, too, whose job it is to explain why New York City public schools deliver subpar results for so much money.

The real scandal of the New York City schools, however, emerges when you peer into its depths and see just how poorly the schools do when it comes to educating black and

Latino students—ostensibly the focus of so much of the city's resources, energy, and rhetoric. Only 28 percent of black kids in the fourth and eighth grades were found to be "proficient" in math, and only 35 percent were proficient in English language arts (ELA). Latino students do a little better, but not by much, with 33 percent marked as proficient in math and almost 37 percent in ELA. The "performance gap" between black and Latino students on the one hand and white students on the other yawns wide. Twice as many white kids are proficient in math and nearly the same amount are proficient in ELA as their black and Latino classmates.

This performance gap is not unique to New York City—it is found nationwide. More than 50 years of sociological study and billions of dollars in resources have gone into figuring out how to close the performance gap between blacks and whites and demonstrate the equality of outcome that equality of opportunity is supposed to produce. So far, no good.

New York City did not suddenly discover the problem of racial disparities in educational performance in 2014, when de Blasio took over City Hall. The question has perplexed New York for decades and roiled politics and race relations. For instance, the famous teachers' strike of 1968 was prompted by community control of a mostly black and Puerto Rican school district in Brooklyn. The new board instituted a radical curriculum based around black self-determination, including Swahili lessons. When the local board fired all the white teachers, the union walked out, shutting down the school system for weeks. Finally, the state had to take over direct control of the district's schools.

Bill de Blasio's first elected position was to the local nine-member school board in Brooklyn's District 15 in 1999. He has always identified himself closely with the New York City school system, frequently citing his school board service and constantly identifying himself as a "K through 12 public school parent." In his 2013 campaign for mayor, de Blasio specifically focused on the school system in order to yoke his twin obsessions with racial equity and wealth inequality by promising to establish universal prekindergarten (UPK) and to cover the cost with a tax on wealthy New Yorkers. Expanding the availability of all-day pre-K to all four-year-old children in New York City was not necessarily controversial in itself—though de Blasio tended to overstate the potential positive outcomes—and the idea in principle was backed by the other candidates, especially council speaker Christine Quinn, his chief rival for the nomination. Quinn, who had defeated de Blasio in 2005 in the race to run the city council, had made early childhood education a signature issue and had successfully lobbied the state legislature to make kindergarten mandatory for all five-year-olds.

What was curious about de Blasio was that he made paying for UPK contingent on a special tax on incomes over $500,000. He delighted in going to Chamber of Commerce luncheons and taunting the attendees with his revenue plan. "You might say, 'You have come to the lion's den,'" he told the Association for a Better New York, a pro-business group. "We will be asking people who worked hard and have done well to contribute a little more and make this happen." The proposal went over poorly among the well-heeled audience—which was likely the plan. Michael Bloomberg, then the mayor, commented that de Blasio "wants to drive everyone out of the city" with higher taxes. But de Blasio grasped that for a large segment of Democrat primary voters, purposefully alienating the rich with class-warfare rhetoric was a selling point.

In his inauguration speech on January 1, 2014, the new mayor of New York set forth his vigorous Progressive agenda. He called on the ghosts of socialism past.

> We are called to put an end to economic and social inequalities that threaten to unravel the city we love. And so today, we commit to a new progressive direction in New York. And that same progressive impulse has written our city's history. It's in our DNA.

Summoning the spirits of Franklin Roosevelt, Frances Perkins, and Fiorello LaGuardia—who "championed a progressive income tax"—de Blasio enumerated the many social programs he planned to institute and expand. Paid sick leave, affordable housing, more hospitals, and community health centers would all need to be funded one way or another, but only universal pre-K was attached to a particular revenue stream, in the form of a special tax on the wealthiest New Yorkers.

Laying a supplemental tax on high-income residents isn't something the mayor of New York City can make happen; only the state legislature and the governor can impose income taxes. De Blasio was trying out his electoral mandate for size, looking to see how far his wings would stretch. Not too far, as it turned out: in a routine that they would play out repeatedly, de Blasio's old boss, Governor Andrew Cuomo, would let his former underling make a grab for the cookie jar of power and influence and then yank it away and slap his hand for good measure.

As early as de Blasio's first week in office, Cuomo made it clear that he also wanted universal pre-K for New York and that it was something the state could cover without a special tax aimed at the rich. De Blasio continued, however, to push for all-day prekindergarten—and the assessment on high earners to pay for it—as though he was struggling against mighty forces arrayed against him. It became increasingly clear that the tax was a kind of punishment that the new mayor wanted to dole out to Manhattan's billionaire class. Referring to what he called the "small soy latte analogy," de Blasio said the tax would cost only as much as one effete hot beverage a day, so why the fuss? At a city council hearing about the benefits of UPK held in February 2014, Speaker Melissa Mark-Viverito, public advocate (now state attorney general) Letitia James, education committee chair Danny Dromm, and schools chancellor Carmen Fariña each spoke in support of the tax. The ascendent Progressives clearly believed that getting the program passed without specifically tacking on a tax on the rich would be a failure.

What's so funny about this demand is that rich New Yorkers would be paying for UPK with or without a special assessment on their income over $500,000. New York taxes its residents aggressively and according to a progressive, graduated schedule—meaning that the rich pay proportionately more. In 2015, for instance, the top 1 percent of New Yorkers by adjusted gross income—people who made more than $600,000—paid 46.3 percent of the state's total tax liability, even though they earned 31.9 percent of the total income. The top 10 percent of earners contributed more than 75 percent of the tax revenue. Nobody's crying for the rich, but it's absurd to perpetuate the idea that they aren't already paying for all the social services.

Even though nobody was opposed to bringing in full-day pre-K for all four-year-olds, Carmen Fariña—six weeks into her new job—made some bizarre remarks in the council hearing about the program that caused alert ears to perk up and wonder about her suitability for the post. Councilman Jumaane Williams, questioning Farina about the importance of getting kids acclimated to school early, asked her to comment about something he'd read regarding child development.

> My last question and a comment, as I'm running down the clock, I've read a lot of reports in places where they state they actually can look at the third grade reading scores and see how many prison cells they're going to build. How accurate is that and how does the DOE take that into account with the things that they're doing?

Williams here cites the kind of data point one hears while listening to people who think the moon landing was a hoax. It's the type of infopop that teachers' union advocates trot out to demand more school funding, on the order of bumper stickers that wish the schools had all the money they need and the army had to hold a bake sale. Chancellor Fariña responded, guilelessly, "The grade at which we look at incarceration in the future is third grade. Third-grade reading scores nationally are the grade by which jails are chosen to be built."

It's obvious why advocates like the factoid. It makes it seem urgent to get little kids into preschool immediately, as the only hope to improve their test scores when they turn eight, so as to spare them from a hellish future of illiteracy, crime, and incarceration. For that reason, presumably, the myth has been cited by Hillary Clinton, Colin Powell, National Public Radio, the editorial pages of the *New York Times*, and a host of other politicians, activists, and reporters throughout the years.

But as piquant as it sounds, it's just not true. Peter Leone, former director of the National Center on Education, Disability and Juvenile Justice, has said about this statistic, "It's catchy, and it's bogus." The canard—which vaguely implies that a conspiracy exists to profit from keeping scores down—gained currency during Terry McAuliffe's 2009 run for governor in Virginia, though it had been floating around for at least several years by that point.

Prison construction, in fact, is planned according to a number of factors, including demography, crime rates, sentencing guidelines, and prison crowding—but not elementary school test scores. A 2010 survey by the California Department of Corrections and Rehabilitation (CDCR), which had received multiple inquiries about the topic, found that nowhere in the country are prisons built according to how well eight-year-olds are doing with their homework. "This is an urban myth," said CDCR spokeswoman Terry Thornton. "We have no idea where this originated from."

The rumor persists, however, because it has such value to its retailers. The idea that underperforming readers in the third grade today are the felons and convicts of tomorrow makes pre-K seem a matter of the deepest significance. It's not just a matter of socializing kids for kindergarten, freeing up single moms to work, or—crucially—further enlarging and shoring up the city's huge nonprofit sector and creating a new cadre of unionizable workers. In this Dickensian, de Blasian vision of the world as a profit center for the prison/industrial complex, pre-K is the salvation of our youth.

In any event, UPK was approved by Albany, and Cuomo found the money to pay for it, so there was no need to add a special tax on the city's top earners. The benefits of pre-K are dubious: there is some improvement seen in reading scores among kids who attend it, but those gains usually evaporate by middle school. But the program remains popular among parents and is one of the few achievements of the de Blasio years that can be called successful. Despite its origins as a campaign wedge issue based on inciting class-based hostility, UPK will likely survive de Blasio as his only legacy program.

· · · · · · · · · ·

Carmen Fariña was a long-time teacher, principal, and superintendent in the New York City school system. By all accounts, she was an excellent educator and leader in those roles. But she was over her head in running the entire school system.

One of Michael Bloomberg's major accomplishments in education was centralization of the system under his direct control. Having convinced Albany to give him this authority, he dissolved the local elected district school boards, which had exercised control over grammar and middle schools. This centralized authority was a blow to the power of the UFT, which effectively "owned" many of the local school boards. Bloomberg created a Department of Education and moved it from its home in Brooklyn to the Tweed Courthouse, right behind City Hall, physically signifying its subsidiary position to the mayor. The corporate titan installed Joel Klein, an attorney with no significant background in education, as the new schools chancellor and tasked him with streamlining and professionalizing the system.

Klein and Bloomberg took a data-driven, top-down approach to school management. They did not hesitate to close failing schools by dissolving the staff and structure and then opening multiple small schools in the same building. Klein instituted a system that assigned each school a letter grade based on how well its students performed on standardized tests, attendance, and the year-to-year improvement of low-performing students. Bloomberg and Klein introduced a bonus system that would monetarily reward the best teachers in higher-need schools based largely on test scores.

Carmen Fariña's approach to school leadership was less data oriented, and she tended to believe that she could tell if a school was doing a good job by visiting it and talking to the teachers and students. The chancellor was happy to get rid of the school grades—which the UFT and the principals' union had always found degrading—and reduce the centrality of standardized testing to evaluating school quality. Data were still tracked but reported in a disaggregated manner so as not to stigmatize "under-resourced" schools; tests were altered and other measures jiggered so as to make comparison with the past impossible. De Blasio's mayoralty would be year zero.

Confronting the performance gap brings up all kinds of uncomfortable questions. The questions are usually positioned as a matter of resources and racism. On average, black and Latino kids do worse than white kids on standardized tests; one convenient way to explain this disparity is by blaming it on racism. A common theme among advocates, officials, and the left generally is that New York City's schools are "segregated," but many have gone further, calling them "apartheid schools," generally meaning schools in which 90 percent of the students are either black or Latino. Others, including Congressman Ritchie Torres of the Bronx, have defined apartheid schools as those with less than 1 percent white enrollment.

The term *apartheid*, of course, refers to the brutal system of legalized racial segregation that existed in South Africa from 1948 to 1994. It's to convey the idea that an elite minority population wields the whip over a racial majority. Most New Yorkers would probably wonder what the city's Department of Education—not known as a nest of white supremacy—has in common with a policy of programmatic racial classification and legally enforced social restriction. While New York, like America in general, has divisions of income that sometimes cleave along ethnoracial lines, no well-off black or Latino families in New York are prevented from moving into any neighborhood they can afford. Ethnic enclaves in New York are largely determined by group affinity. Chinese immigrants have gravitated toward communities in Lower Manhattan, Brooklyn's Sunset Park, and Flushing, Queens, but it would be absurd to suggest that Asian Americans in New York are somehow victims of segregation, along the lines of Jim Crow–era Dixie.

The 90 percent black and Latino figure cited by critics sounds alarming, but more than two out of three kids (68 percent) in the city's public school system are black and Latino. It takes only a minimal amount of population concentration for a public school to fall into the apartheid category—in which poor children are concentrated with one another in schools that consign them to "steep disadvantage." Torres complains that "the average black or Latino student attends a school where nearly 70 percent of the students are low-income." But again, context is needed: according to the Department of Education, about 75 percent of all students in the system are poor. And 90 percent of all city public schools have student bodies that are at least 50 percent poor. So it's no surprise that black and Latino kids attend primarily lower-income schools.

Elected officials, the Department of Education, and local ideologues have adopted a cure for New York's apartheid problem in several districts, including Park Slope and the Upper West Side, which have a combination of racial diversity and a vocally left-wing white population dedicated to the idea of engineering a more just society, starting with revising middle school admissions policies. They have removed all admission "screens," including attendance and tardiness records—which are considered racist and classist—report card grades and test scores, and auditions or interviews.

The District 15 Diversity Plan, covering Bill de Blasio's former district in Brooklyn, aims to achieve 52 percent low-income, English-learning, and homeless student penetration in every school as a means of destroying apartheid in the schools. This could work in a few racially diverse and politically "woke" New York City neighborhoods, but what about other parts of the city? The student population of the Bronx, for instance, is already 90 percent black and Latino. Even the most authoritarian social planner, carefully relocating the borough's few white and Asian students, would never be able to achieve nonapartheid status for more than a few schools, and only then at the expense of others. Or consider Staten Island, whose student body is almost half white and which accounts on its own for about 20 percent of the school system's white population. Would the white children of Staten Island's South Shore have to take buses, ferries, and subways out to remote corners of New York City to satisfy the vision of racial equity?

The logic behind the assertion that most of the schools are apartheid schools is faulty because Gotham is a "majority-minority" city. The school system roughly maps to the same population concentrations that are found throughout the city. It's no surprise to anyone that the Upper East Side and Greenwich Village are mostly white, that Corona is Latino, and that East New York is mostly black. It's also no surprise that many white children attend private or religious schools, especially tens of thousands of Orthodox Jews in Brooklyn, thus skewing the demographics of the public school population and making it that much more difficult to achieve an idealized racial balance.

The assumption behind all of this discussion of school seg-regation in New York City is that white students are an unfairly distributed resource who need to be spread around for the benefit of everyone. In some manner—never explained—nonwhite students can thrive only if they are in proximity to white kids. But at only 15 percent of the total student body, there will never be enough whites to go around. Talking about "separate and unequal" schools abuses language in the service of ideology. Arguments can be made about inequi-table funding for education at the state level or about fund-ing disparities between urban and suburban schools, but all schools within New York City receive roughly the same level of funding from the Department of Education, which appor-tions money based on a rigorous per-student formula.

Carmen Fariña retired at the end of de Blasio's first term, and her replacement, Richard Carranza, represented the total capitulation of the New York City school system to the principle of equity over excellence. Carranza was not the mayor's first choice. In February 2018 he announced that Alberto Carvalho, the superintendent of Miami-Dade County's school system, had accepted the job. But within a day, Carvalho pulled out, supposedly because de Blasio refused to let him pick his own subordinates.

Carranza, the superintendent of the Houston schools, immediately began insulting New York parents. He tweeted out a link to a video headlined, "WATCH: WEALTHY WHITE MANHATTAN PARENTS ANGRILY RANT AGAINST PLAN TO BRING MORE BLACK KIDS TO THEIR SCHOOLS." The video showed a sensitive debate about plans to engineer a new racial balance in three Upper

West Side middle schools; casting the complicated discussion as a "rant" against "black kids" on the part of "wealthy white Manhattan parents" was typical of tabloid-style clickbait.

One would think that the new head of the country's largest school system would not want to blast out incendiary messages designed to foment racial hostility. But Carranza made such utterances part of his brand. When a white woman told Carranza on a radio call-in show that she was "stunned" by his statement and "hear loud and clear—me as a white parent in P.S. 199—I am not part of your constituency," the chancellor advised her to attend implicit-bias training classes. He was telling her to check her privilege, as the saying goes, before speaking to him again.

Carranza has continued to spread his radical, race-based message of transformation. "We're not about improving the system," he told Al Sharpton's National Action Network last weekend. "We're about changing the system." That system, he claims, fails to teach black and Latino students while offering a different level of service to other, presumably white children. Carranza has pushed to eliminate the test-based system of admission to the city's specialized high schools, which has resulted in wildly disproportionate representation of South Asian and East Asian kids in Brooklyn Tech, Stuyvesant, and six other premier schools. "I don't buy into the narrative that any one ethnic group owns admissions to these schools," Carranza said, as though studying for and excelling on standardized tests is a statement of racial exclusivity.

Carranza instituted antibias training throughout the Department of Education—who could oppose fairness? But *bias* is construed narrowly to mean "white-supremacy culture," which must be eradicated from the hearts and minds of New York's public school teachers, not usually the population one associates with virulent racial movements. As part of Carranza's wide-ranging initiative to eradicate racism from the public school system, he hired consultants to conduct intensive antibias trainings with educators. One consultant, Darnisa Amante, explained that giving middle-class black children more attention and resources than poor white children is just and necessary "because over the course of his lifetime he will have less access and less opportunities than that poor white boy. That's what racial equity is." Another presentation about the elements of white supremacy culture that was given to administrators included "perfectionism," "worship of the written word," and "objectivity" as aspects of white supremacy that must be removed root and branch from New York City's classrooms.

I asked Richard Carranza and Bill de Blasio once, because implicit bias training is so important, to offer moments from their own personal experience when they were forced to confront biased attitudes in their own minds. The mayor didn't like the question and refused to offer specifics, growing testy when pressed on it. Chancellor Carranza loved the question, explaining, "I went to a school in Tucson, Arizona, where probably 96 percent of the student body looked like me." But when he went to college, he found himself in

classes with people from a European heritage, people that had blond hair that had been to private schools. My implicit bias was that they were smarter than me, they were better prepared than me to succeed in college, and there was sort of an implicit inferiority complex that I brought with me.

But then by graduating from college and doing so well, he learned that white people are not actually better than he is. Carranza's experience with intrinsic bias about race has taught him only that he should have as much self-esteem as he wants, because any doubt is likely just an inferiority complex foisted on him by the culture of white supremacy.

Critical race theory and the doctrine of "equity," which has perverted the principle of equality of opportunity into a demand that immutable characteristics such as race determine place in society, are destructive ideologies that are contrary to every principle of justice. The Progressive ascendency has pushed resolutely to destroy standards of excellence, merit-based reward, and the incentive of achievement among New York City's youth.

9

Systemic Rot: How Reform Became Corruption

WITH NEW YORK CITY suffering so badly, it was natural for people to number the days left until de Blasio's term would be over and we could get a new mayor to repair the damage. Surely the obvious crisis in leadership could be cured by electing a better leader. Unfortunately, it's not that easy.

As I hope this book has demonstrated, Bill de Blasio is a symptom of deep, underlying rot. He's a useful target because he's so peevish, ineffectual, and addicted to displays of self-righteous grandiosity. But New York's problems go well beyond the laziness, stubbornness, and bad ideas of any one individual politician. The city needs a great deal of work if it hopes to pull itself out of the muck into which it is currently sinking.

A series of reforms to the political and electoral system in New York, which were supposed to expand democracy, appears to have had the opposite effect. In the mayoral election of 1953, 93 percent of registered voters came to the polls; in 2017, that figure had fallen to less than 22 percent. The last time so few people—just over 1 million—turned out to vote for mayor was 1917—before women's suffrage doubled the electorate.

New York City used to be run by political machines that rewarded supporters through patronage in the form of jobs. Over the course of time, reformers—especially during the original Progressive movement, around the time of World War I—instituted changes in government staffing. Before, a change in political leadership could mean that everyone who worked for the government lost his or her job, from teachers to sanitation workers to actuaries. This manifest inefficiency led to introduction of the civil service and the advent of professional, apolitical administration.

While letting councilmen pick the local dogcatcher and lamplighter was a corrupt way to handle municipal hiring, it did mean that elected officials and their constituents had a symbiotic, responsive relationship. Voting was of consequence, because if your candidate lost, you lost your job. Even after the decline of the most blatant forms of patronage, local political clubs—which persist in some neighborhoods as a shadow of their former selves—retained significant power and bound elected officials tightly to their communities.

Today, most New Yorkers don't know who their local representatives are, and they don't care. And for good reason, because most elected officials effectively win their seats in the primary election, which attracts much lower turnout than the general election and is driven by a narrow set of issues that most potential voters would find baffling or meaningless.

Nationally, people complain about the two-party system as constraining and offering a false choice. But at least a two-party system provides for some pushback or give-and-take. Democrats and Republicans may run to the extremes in the primary, but they know that they will have to answer for their fringe statements in the general, so they tend to modulate their voices accordingly. But New York City—like most big cities in America—operates as a one-party state. Out of 51 council seats, 48 are occupied by Democrats; perhaps one or two are swing seats. There are 65 state assembly seats filled from New York City, and 63 are held by Democrats. Out of 24 state senate seats from the city, 23 are Democrat held. And out of 11 US congressional seats, Democrats solidly hold all but one, which tends to flip back and forth.

What this means is that the primary election is usually the real contest, though the primaries have even lower turnout than the general. And because there is no concern about alienating centrist voters or activating the other side in November by being too extreme early on, the result is that candidates tend to play to the fringes of the party, which in New York means the far left. As a result, candidates leapfrog each other in staking out ever more radical positions to appeal to the activist base, which is more ideologically attuned than the average voter and more likely to punish candidates who deviate even slightly from extreme positions.

For example, until recently, it would have been outlandish to suggest that prostitution—"sex work"—should be legalized. But in a November 2020 forum, five of seven candidates, including two of the leading contenders, agreed that it should not have criminal penalties. But beyond that, the so-called Nordic model—which views prostitutes as victims and prosecutes their clients—is now held to be regressive and unduly harsh because how are prostitutes expected to make money if their johns are afraid to hire them? Hence, the candidates mostly favor nonprosecution of either party.

The situation is similar in the vigorous contest to replace Cy Vance, the Manhattan district attorney. With crime soaring and QoL plummeting, one would expect candidates to be running on a theme of restoring law and order. But in line with a frightening and seemingly inexorable national pattern, most of the people running are committed to keeping as many people out of jail as possible, even for serious crimes. In cities across the country there is a concerted, coordinated effort afoot to decriminalize supposed "crimes of poverty," which means nonprosecution of "low-level offenses" resulting from addiction, homelessness, or being poor.

A tough-on-crime prosecutor could run a no-nonsense campaign advocating for victims and safe streets, of course. But the nature of the Democratic primary system is that anyone who runs even slightly to the right of the field gets cast as a rabid right-wing bootlicker. The number of people in jail in Manhattan is at a historic low, but almost all the candidates say it's not low enough. This is the logic of "progress" as a political principle: we are aiming at perfection, but our prior efforts have been insufficient; thus we must redouble our commitment. The "leapfrog" nature of the dynamic encourages everyone to shift the median position further to the left. Yesterday's radical firebrand becomes today's tepid centrist, and today's moderate will be tomorrow's reactionary.

This same dynamic works regarding the electorate. The "Curley effect," named for four-term mayor of Boston James Michael Curley, describes the way in which politicians—as Bertolt Brecht said—"elect a new people." Curley was an Irish Catholic who found the legacy WASP elite of Boston an unfortunate hindrance to perpetual rule by him and his coreligionists. The powerful Curley used tax revenue to build playgrounds and other amenities in Irish neighborhoods and permitted burlesque houses to open in traditionally Protestant districts, whose potholed streets would go unrepaired. He widely expanded public employment among his preferred constituents and cut the pay of school doctors and other elites. Curley specialized in insulting the legacy Anglo-Saxon population of Boston while praising the "newer and better America" represented by more recently arrived Irish immigrants. The strategy worked. The Brahmins left, and Boston has not had a Protestant mayor—and only one non-Irish mayor—in almost 100 years.

Sound familiar? The strategy has been put into effect—with different players—in many cities. In New York City, the racial politics are more complex, but suffice to say that residents of any race who prefer not to live in a city with high taxes, significant homelessness, and politicians who favor dismantling the police may find it easier to leave than to stay and fight. People who tolerate the politics of racial resentment, onerous business regulations, and a school system dedicated to equity over excellence stick it out. Over time, the electorate is shaped by the elected.

Term limits, which are always touted as a way to open up a sclerotic system of elected officials who take their positions for granted, only encourage this leftward drift. The 2021 election will clear out the city council almost en masse—40 out of 51 councilmembers are term limited. This creates a mad rush of candidates jockeying to distinguish themselves as more radically committed to social justice than each other. Again, there's no objective reason why candidates running to make safer streets and improve the business climate couldn't emerge as leaders—it's just not likely to happen.

One reason for this is that most elected officials in New York City get their training, funding, and institutional support from working as political staffers, in government, or from the nonprofit world. As such, they pass their adult years in a culture of faith in government to answer all the fundamental problems of life. Their professional and social lives are spent with similarly minded activists, all of whom consume the same media and align themselves along similar channels of Progressive Democratic politics. Their colleagues in the hothouse of community board politics, Democratic clubs, community education councils, state party committee conventions, and protest march planning sessions are acutely attuned to deviations in acceptable opinion, and aspirants in that world quickly learn self-discipline in how they speak and what not to say.

Very few elected officials in New York City today have much private-sector experience. Many of them, like Mayor de Blasio, spent their most significant years of professional life as staffers to elected officials or working on campaigns. This is where they learn about intergovernmental relations, the importance of cultivating friends and allies in the labor movement, how to associate with powerful political consultants, and the ins and outs of election law, including petitioning to get on the ballot and—as important—how to get your rivals thrown off the ballot. Owning a business, being a professional, or simply working as an employee for a company may inform you about life as it is lived for most people, but it will not teach you anything about how to run for office.

As part of a major reform package that de Blasio signed, the city council gave itself a substantial 32 percent pay raise in 2016. In exchange, the role of being a councilmember was turned into a "full-time job," meaning that the members were no longer permitted to earn outside income. But it is not unfair to note that most of them wouldn't be able to earn outside income anyway because they are to a large extent inexperienced at work outside the public sector. A councilmember can't legitimately have a second job working as a chief of staff for another councilmember, after all.

One councilmember, Ydanis Rodriguez, expressed discontent that the pay hike wasn't more substantial. After all, he pointed out, he works "more than full-time," going to local meetings, schmoozing with constituents, attending banquets, etc. None of that work is considered on-the-clock, yet he doesn't receive time-and-a-half for putting in all that overtime.

It is said that personnel is policy—those whom you hire to staff your organization will define the organization, its mission, and the execution of its goals. People who go to work for New York City government in a policy capacity— whether as staff for elected officials, in City Hall, or in city agencies—do not come to these jobs as nonpartisan, disinterested functionaries dedicated to efficient, good government in the model of Woodrow Wilson's 1887 treatise, "The Study of Administration." They are ideologically committed to a radical vision of social justice, which by no means conflicts with or impedes their careerism; in fact, doctrinal orthodoxy is a precondition of professional advancement.

Erin Drinkwater, a deputy commissioner of intergovernmental and legislative affairs at the Department of Social Services, typifies the professional activist staffing city agencies. Drinkwater made waves when she represented her agency in meetings with the community board on the Upper West Side regarding the policy of moving hundreds of homeless men into local hotels, in response to the COVID-19 crisis. Homeless advocates, both in and out of government, used the pandemic as grounds to advance their most radical proposals to end congregate shelters and move homeless people into permanent housing, almost overnight. This issue became a flashpoint on the famously tolerant Upper West Side, with local elected officials accusing their constituents of being white supremacists for complaining about a spike in random street assaults.

During a contentious Zoom meeting in August, where members of the neighborhood complained about an explosion in street crime, public drug use and sex, and violence, Drinkwater spoke blandly about compassionate emergency responses to the pandemic—though many of the 700 relocated homeless people had simply been moved out of hotels in other neighborhoods where they were causing QoL problems, too—and refused to answer direct questions about the future status of the hotels. Shortly after the meeting, she tweeted, "Comfort the afflicted; afflict the comfortable."

Questioned about her meaning, Drinkwater said it was from the Bible—it is not—and explained that she saw the motto as expressing the need for people with privileged lives to reflect on their responsibilities to the less fortunate. Many members of the community were amazed to see a high-level public official proclaim that she sees it as her duty to "afflict" the citizenry, whose "comfort" is an affront to the cause of social justice. But this sentiment, though clumsily expressed, really defines the principle of equity, a goal of which is making sure that everyone is equally miserable.

Before working for the city government, Erin Drinkwater had "been deeply embedded in progressive politics and social justice campaigns," according to a 2014 profile in *Go* magazine. She was executive director of the Brooklyn Community Pride Center,

served in leadership roles with Empire State Pride Agenda and Lambda Independent Democrats; as Congressman Jerrold L. Nadler's Manhattan Community Representative and LGBT Liaison; and as Sean Patrick Maloney's Policy Director in his 2006 Attorney General bid. More recently, she worked on the two Obama for America campaigns and was chosen as a delegate to the 2012 DNC Convention.

Not to overstate the importance of a functionary—just a cog in the Prog—but Erin Drinkwater is the model of a contemporary professional activist. Shuttling between political campaigns, nonprofit organizations, and positions in government, Drinkwater personifies the hidden administrative elite that maintains a kind of permanent control over the direction of policy, regardless of who's in office. To borrow a term from national politics, we may postulate the existence of a municipal deep state that exists in the marrow of city agencies, civil society institutions, media, and politics.

In September 2018, activist groups around New York rushed to denounce the Trump administration for considering changes to the "public charge" rule for noncitizens. The changes would add food stamps, Medicaid, and federal housing vouchers to the programs that count against immigrants when the government determines their future status. The New York Immigration Coalition (NYIC) staged a protest outside the Tenement Museum on the Lower East Side, joined by the African Services Committee and the Chinese-American Planning Council. Executives of the three organizations were arrested after they sat down in the middle of Delancey Street and blocked rush-hour traffic.

New York City has long been fertile ground for political protest, of course, so these events were not unusual. Civil society groups, along with elected officials, activists, and unions, typically organize these protests, which run the gamut from standard political rallies to civil disobedience. What most New Yorkers don't realize, though, is that many of the protests, including NYIC's action last year, aren't simply the work of civic-minded private citizens. On the contrary: they are funded, sometimes lavishly, by local and state government—that is, by taxpayers. New York is home to a host of such groups, which have expanded their charitable missions to include near-constant political activism. Whether they agree or disagree with these efforts, New Yorkers should understand that they're paying the bill for them.

New York City spends about $95 billion annually. Not counting Medicaid spending, the city allocates about 13 percent of its outlays to human services—including homeless shelters, senior centers, youth recreation, adult literacy, foster care, and many other programs. The city contracts with nonprofit organizations to provide many of these services. Most homeless shelters are run by nongovernmental organizations. Similarly, nonprofits provide public defenders to indigent defendants. Individual contracts with these large groups—such as the Lutheran Social Services of Metropolitan New York, Inc., which deals with vulnerable children—can run to hundreds of millions of dollars annually.

Any nonprofit receiving money from the city is supposed to have a purely charitable purpose, though the boundaries between philanthropy and politics can be fuzzy. Organizations that engage in electoral politics, for instance, can't receive funding, though funded groups can run voter registration campaigns. It's no surprise that politically well-connected groups—those that can afford to hire lobbyists and consultants, employ former elected officials as executives and engage at the highest levels of political socializing and contributorship—tend to receive large shares of city funding.

A significant recipient of taxpayer largesse, receiving about $9 million annually, is Make the Road New York, which, according to its website, "builds the power of Latino and working class communities to achieve dignity and justice through organizing, policy innovation, transformative education, and survival services." Founded by attorneys Andrew Friedman and Oona Chatterjee in 1997, Make the Road characterizes itself as a member-driven organization with more than 15,000 New York City members, almost exclusively Latino immigrants. The group receives millions of dollars in city and state funding annually, ostensibly to run adult literacy classes, "know your rights" clinics, cultural activities, and assorted information sessions.

But Make the Road's real purpose, to paraphrase its mission statement, is to "build power through organizing." Leaders of the Working Families Party run the group, which urges its clients to participate in political indoctrination as an implicit condition of receiving aid and encourages them to join as members. Make the Road's legal structure and leadership closely overlap with Make the Road Action—a 501(c)(4) organization that legally engages in electoral activity and endorsing candidates—to which Make the Road regularly makes contributions in the six-figure range. New York Communities for Change, the successor organization to the disgraced ACORN, also receives money from Make the Road. Friedman and Chatterjee spun off a larger national organization, the

Center for Popular Democracy, which receives millions of dollars in donations from the George Soros–funded Open Society Foundations, the Ford Foundation, organized labor, and the Rockefeller Foundation—and which operates from the same street address as Make the Road Action, with which it shares overlapping leadership.

Public funding thus fuels an interlocking complex of political organizations on the left, including direct electoral endorsements and campaign work. Democratic elected officials know that they can count on Make the Road to thicken crowds at rallies and stand behind them at press appearances. When Mayor de Blasio announced that he would not permit ICE agents to enter public school buildings, he was surrounded by Make the Road members; when he visited Las Vegas in April, as part of his preannouncement presidential tour, he met with Make the Road Nevada.

Other nonprofits operate in a similar politicized mode. The election of Donald Trump and the resulting resistance to it erased the old rules that kept publicly funded social services providers from behaving like political factions. For instance, one week after Trump's inauguration, NYIC, joining forces with Make the Road, organized a march to protest the administration's "Muslim ban." NYIC posted a video showing the leaders of the march holding a large banner reading, "No ban, no wall!," with Make the Road and NYIC signs attached. Congressional representatives Joe Crowley and Nydia Velázquez led the marchers in chanting, "Hey hey, ho ho / Donald Trump has got to go!"

Later in 2017, NYIC and African Communities Together, which received a grant from the publicly supported

Communities of Color Nonprofit Stabilization Fund, joined a protest outside Trump Tower in honor of World Refugee Day. Blocking the sidewalk and spilling into the street, the protesters chanted, "No hate, no fear / Refugees are welcome here." When in January 2018 ICE took into custody Ravi Ragbir—a Trinidadian immigrant with a felony conviction for wire fraud in connection with a subprime mortgage scam—to be deported, New York's social justice protest complex swung into action. NYIC and Make the Road, among others, issued immediate calls for action, and protesters, including elected officials, caused a melee on lower Broadway, blocking emergency vehicles.

The next month, ICE arrested an illegal immigrant, who was facing a felony domestic violence complaint, outside the Bronx criminal courthouse. Lawyers from the Legal Aid Society and Bronx Defenders—both publicly funded, to the tune of tens of millions of dollars annually—staged a walkout from their cases and stood outside chanting, "Say it loud, say it clear / Immigrants are welcome here." These groups are, legally speaking, charitable organizations—funded almost entirely by the taxpayer—that are supposed to provide indigent defense, not to protest federal immigration policy.

At least the public-defender groups can argue that ICE impedes their work when it arrests illegal immigrants on their way to court. But when Make the Road organizes protests outside Wells Fargo, Goldman Sachs, and JPMorgan Chase—"corporations that stand to benefit from Trump's anti-immigrant, anti-worker policies"—it's harder to make the case that the group is pursuing its supposed charitable mission of helping immigrants learn English or get healthcare. Make the Road led the fight to prevent Amazon from locating a corporate headquarters in Queens. "This is a huge victory. We are thrilled," exulted Make the Road coexecutive director Deborah Axt after the tech giant pulled out, deciding that the headache wasn't worth it.

The nomination of Brett Kavanaugh to the Supreme Court drew intense opposition from New York's politicized nonprofit world. NYIC sponsored a protest, marching on the Yale Club in midtown Manhattan (Kavanaugh attended Yale). But it wasn't just NYIC. On the first day of Kavanaugh's Judiciary Committee confirmation hearings—before any allegations of sexual assault by the nominee had been made public—70 people were arrested inside the chamber for disruptive behavior. Their actions were clearly coordinated, as each protester waited until the previous one was dragged out before shouting imprecations at the nominee. The first protester was Linda Sarsour, nationally prominent as a cohead of the Women's March but also a long-time fixture in New York City protest politics as the executive director of the Arab American Association of New York. Generously funded by taxpayers, her organization offers language classes and naturalization preparation and pursues "law enforcement accountability" and an end to "discriminatory policing practices."

Later in the confirmation cycle, after accusations of sexual assault had been leveled against Kavanaugh, two women captured national headlines when they confronted Senator Jeff Flake in an elevator, screaming that they had been raped, in an effort to get him to vote against the nominee. Media celebrated the women, but it's noteworthy that the older of the two, and the leader, was Ana Maria Archila, coexecutive director of the Center for Popular Democracy, who, apparently, still served as executive director of Make the Road: it is her signature that appears, on the line marked "President," on the organization's state filing dated October 20, 2018—a few weeks after her elevator encounter.

Sarsour and Archila are professional activists, skilled organizers, and adept at seizing the dramatic moment. Their training was honed through well-compensated work for what are ostensibly municipal social services providers that really function as taxpayer-funded cadres for social justice activism. These left-wing groups develop talent that goes on to run political campaigns, work for elected officials, staff government agencies, and run for elected office. New York's multibillion-dollar human services complex generally provides the aid that it promises, but it has also become the operating environment for radicals, posing as social workers, who siphon off public money to promote their political agenda.

· · · · · · · · · ·

The idea that electing a new mayor is going to save New York from the Prog looks faintly ridiculous when you consider everything I have laid out over the preceding chapters. But if you are still cleaving to that hope, ask yourself, Who? Let's survey the current leadership of the city and state and also consider the "bench" of up-and-comers.

Governor Andrew Cuomo presided over the most disastrous state response to the COVID-19 pandemic in the nation, and possibly the world, while at the same time receiving national praise from elite sources for his heroic response. At least 12,000, and possibly as many as 15,000, residents of nursing homes died because Cuomo—worried that the hospital system would get flooded—ordered that care facilities admit contagious patients. At the time, in March of 2020, little was understood about the virus, and Cuomo might deserve the benefit of the doubt if he hadn't spent the rest of the year presenting himself as a national savior, including writing a book about his own stellar leadership.

Throughout the course of the pandemic, the governor gave daily televised briefings in which he hailed his performance as a beacon of leadership and savior of the country. Cuomo delivered such bocce-court apothegms as, "It's going to be hard, there is no doubt. But at the same time it is going to be OK." He also made a point, continuously, of calling the novel coronavirus the "European virus," presumably in counterpoint to Trump's implicit racism in calling it the "China virus," even though it is beyond dispute that the virus originated in China, even if some infected people may have caught it in Italy before bringing it to America.

The media swooned over his "wisdom and competence," in the words of former Trump staffer turned arch-opponent Anthony Scaramucci. His "competence is captivating," said the *New York Times*. Reporter Carl Bernstein, who used a disgruntled FBI source to help bring down Richard Nixon, praised Cuomo's "real leadership," and actor and prominent Democrat Mark Ruffalo said that "New Yorkers are lucky to have a leader like Governor Cuomo in this crisis." In April, at the peak of the crisis, Cuomo appeared on Ellen DeGeneres's popular television show to announce that he approved of the use of the word "Cuomosexual," embraced by DeGeneres and her fellow talk show hosts Stephen Colbert and Trevor Noah, to describe people who love him.

Cuomo also appeared almost every night on his brother Chris Cuomo's show on CNN. The two brothers frequently bantered about whose nose was bigger, who was more devoted to their mother in faithfully reproducing her recipe for sauce, and how well the "Luv Guv," in journalist Chris Cuomo's words, had done in serving the state of New York. "Obviously I love you as a brother, obviously I'll never be objective, obviously I think you're the best politician in the country," enthused the award-winning news analyst.

In November 2020, Governor Cuomo was presented with his own special Emmy for his television appearances. Bruce Paisner, CEO of the International Academy of Television Arts and Sciences, presented the award to Cuomo.

> Last spring, when the virus was new and out of control, and the people of New York were frightened at its relentless spread, one man took it upon himself to use technology to spread reliable information and tell citizens what to do. Governor Cuomo's daily press conferences were a whole new dimension in public education. He informed, he demanded, and he calmed people down.

In January 2021 it emerged that—as right-leaning media sources had reported for nearly six months, despite stonewalling from Albany—the actual nursing home death toll was double Cuomo's estimates. In reaction to this news, the Emmy winner snapped, "Who cares? 33 [percent], 28 [percent]. Died in a hospital. Died in a nursing home. They died."

Before COVID-19, Cuomo presided over economic development schemes for depressed and depopulated upstate New York—including $15 million to launch a Syracuse Film Hub—that were virtually a complete waste. In 2013 Cuomo launched START-UP NY, a program that created tax-free zones for new companies in certain industries in depressed areas. After four years of operation, the program had created an estimated 722 new net jobs, in a state where private employment is over 7 million. START-UP NY was rolled out with great fanfare and a $47 million marketing campaign.

Joseph Percoco was Andrew Cuomo's long-time closest advisor, best friend, and the man he called his "father's third son" at the funeral of Mario Cuomo. Percoco was found guilty of taking bribes—which he called "ziti" as a clumsy codeword in phone conversations—in exchange for selling his influence with state government and was sentenced to six years in federal prison. The governor's new closest aide, Melissa DeRosa, is the daughter of Giorgio DeRosa, a partner at Bolton-St. Johns, one of the state's largest and most important lobbying firms. Her siblings work there, too, and her husband became a top executive at Uber at the same time that the company was seeking to expand its New York presence.

Cuomo hasn't been personally accused of venality, but in his efforts to vacuum up campaign contributions, he hasn't let much stand in his way. Despite a 2007 executive order forbidding political appointees from donating to the governor who appointed them, Cuomo has accepted hundreds of thousands of dollars from such appointees and hundreds of thousands more from their wives, children, and associated business entities. Though the governor ran for reelection in 2014 promising to sweep out Albany's Augean stables of filth, he shut down his good-government Moreland Commission to Investigate Public Corruption when it took what to him was a wrong turn. When the commission started looking into a state vendor who had donated to Cuomo's campaign, the governor quickly shut it down.

"It's my commission," explained Cuomo, in the calm terms of any madman. "My subpoena power, my Moreland Commission. I can appoint it, I can disband it. I appoint you, I can un-appoint you tomorrow. . . . It's my commission. I can't 'interfere' with it, because it is mine. It is controlled by me." This kind of grandiose language characterizes Cuomo's approach to governance. He vowed to lead a flotilla of plea-sure craft to block off-shore drilling, should it be autho-rized, "just as Winston Churchill did in Dunkirk. ... If you think I'm kidding, I'm not, and I'm going to lead that citizen fleet." Cuomo also promised to sue the Supreme Court if it overturned *Roe v. Wade*, though he didn't specify the venue where he would file that case.

In his first two terms, Cuomo presided over a divided gov-ernment, with the state senate controlled by the Republicans and the assembly in the hands of the Democrats. This arrangement gave Cuomo immense power as a power broker. Even after the Democrats won the upper chamber in 2018, Cuomo was able to present himself as the mod-erate bulwark against radical downstate craziness. But in 2020, the Democrats achieved veto-proof majorities in both houses, essentially sidelining the governor, who could no longer push the legislature around. The statewide Progressive agenda can now accelerate downhill until the wheels unthread themselves entirely.

A likely successor to Cuomo in Albany is Attorney General Letitia James. She replaced the former attorney general, her fellow WFP hero and standard bearer, Eric Schneiderman, who had to resign after it emerged that he liked to beat up his sex partners, an open secret in New York Democratic politics for years. James, a close ally to Governor Cuomo, had previously served as New York City public advocate and as a council member.

While in the city council in 2009, James was trying to cross the street between two cars and bumped into a trailer hitch protruding from a laborer's truck, which was legally parked. Claiming she suffered "great physical and mental pain," she filed suit against the owner of the truck, who earned a living by toting recyclable cans and doing similar odd jobs. Her personal injury lawsuit claimed that her injuries left her unable to work, even though the incident occurred in the middle of her primary election campaign, which she fought and won.

Later in 2009, the night before Veterans' Day, thousands of teenagers gathered on Fulton Mall in Brooklyn, in James's council district. There were fights, two shootings, and a stabbing. Letitia James blamed Buffalo Wild Wings, a local restaurant whose regular Tuesday night 40-cent chicken wing special represented "poor planning" and "irresponsible management." James slammed Buffalo Wild Wings for "failing to provide adequate security" the night before a school holiday. "I want this Tuesday restaurant promotion stopped, or the lease of this business revoked," James said.

Similarly, as attorney general, James sued to dissolve the National Rifle Association on the grounds that it is "fraught with fraud and abuse." She made this announcement in August 2020, in the middle of a 177 percent increase in shootings over the previous year. In both cases, James sought to deflect blame for street violence away from the perpetrators and onto national organizations she claimed to be irresponsibly injuring inner-city communities. In September 2020, in response to the 2019 NYPD shooting of Allan Feliz, a motorist who was attempting to drive away from a traffic stop, putting the lives of the officers at risk, Attorney General James said that the police should stop making traffic stops—even of drivers with outstanding arrest warrants—in order to "limit the likelihood of the kind of escalation" that resulted in the shooting of Feliz, even though it was found to be legally justified.

James also pursued civil litigation against ExxonMobil, claiming that fossil fuel companies had "defrauded" their investors by using two different estimates of the cost per ton of carbon emissions. James demanded monetary relief for investors who had been injured by the company's actions and injunctive relief that would essentially permit her office—in the form of an "independent monitor"—to oversee ExxonMobil's operations. A judge found that James had not proven that ExxonMobil had violated any aspect of securities law, and according to the *Wall Street Journal*, "The AG didn't depose a single investor who claimed to have been duped, and even her witnesses supported Exxon."

"Love trumps Trump's trump," announced Public Advocate Letitia James, without further elaboration, at a rally against

Donald Trump's "Muslim ban" in early 2017. This inane comment predicted her campaign for attorney general, which was based almost entirely around the promise to prosecute Trump. "I will be shining a bright light into every dark corner of his real estate dealings, and every dealing, demanding truthfulness at every turn," James announced on the night of her victory. Since taking office, that's been the bulk of her work. Peering into the massive, documented political corruption throughout New York State, which involves her allies and important Democrat donors, has not emerged as a significant concern.

The most famous legislator in New York, if not the country, is Representative Alexandria Ocasio-Cortez, who is considered to have a shining political future. She is talked up as the next senator, mayor, governor, or even as a future president. Immediately styled with her own triliteral, like FDR or JFK, AOC enjoys rock star appeal—so much so that she has made it clear that electoral politics may not even be big enough for the likes of her. "I don't even know if I want to be in politics," AOC said. "You know, for real, in the first six months of my term, I didn't even know if I was going to run for reelection this year." What gratitude to her constituents, who elevated a bartender to international renown.

Ocasio-Cortez speaks constantly of her chops as an expert on economics—having majored in the subject—but seems to flub certain basics of supply and demand, not to mention cause and effect. She celebrated when Amazon declined to locate its headquarters in Queens and demanded that the $3 billion in tax breaks the state had offered the megacorporation now be used to fund schools and fix the subways;

of course, that money was promised against future tax revenue, which would now not be generated in the first place.

AOC talks like this all the time. "No one ever makes a billion dollars," she said. "You take a billion dollars." But it's not clear why, if that's true, it doesn't hold for lesser amounts as well. By her logic, can't it be said that no one ever makes a thousand dollars, without taking it from someone else? She also suggested that the city's rise in murder and shootings is, at base, an economic problem.

> Maybe this has to do with the fact that people aren't paying their rent and are scared to pay their rent and so they go out and they need to feed their child and they don't have money so you maybe have to . . . they are put in a position where they feel they either need to shoplift some bread or go hungry that night.

This explanation comes straight from *Les Misérables*, and it remains a popular view about why crime occurs: all crime is economic at root. Calls to defund the police and transfer the money spent on law enforcement to social services reflect this sentiment. Spending enough money on social workers, food banks, housing, and education would render police obsolete because crime would vanish.

Of course, it's inconvenient to point out that murder in New York City is not driven by economic need. Few, if any, killings appear to have been the result of a "robbery gone wrong." These are acts of revenge or score settling, not economic crimes of opportunity. Ocasio-Cortez's vision of crime as driven by the need for bread is satisfyingly simple because if it were true, it would be easy to fix.

Scott Stringer, a leading candidate for mayor, is the city comptroller; thus, he signed off on all of de Blasio's budgets. As the supposed financial watchdog for New York City, he spent two terms criticizing the mayor for not spending more money or expanding social services rapidly enough. As one of dozens such examples, he issued a report in September 2019 called, "Fees, Fines and Fairness: How Monetary Charges Drive Inequity in New York City's Criminal Justice System," demanding waivers on fines based on inability to pay. As a Jewish candidate, he has played up his support for Israel at the same time that he has actively sought the endorsement of hardline socialist anti-Zionists in the Democratic Socialists of America.

Stringer claims to have a solution to the housing crunch in New York City. Currently, property developers are allowed to build new housing on land they own or lease as long as it comports with existing laws on code and zoning. This is called "as-of-right development." If a developer seeks an exemption from the land use rules in order to build a bigger building than the law permits, then he or she usually has to strike a deal with the city to subsidize some of the proposed units and reserve them as "affordable" for people who otherwise could not afford to move into a brand-new building at the market rate. These subsidized units are typically geared toward people who earn near the area median income (AMI).

Most new building in New York City is as-of-right. Stringer wants to eliminate as-of-right development, insert city planners into virtually all new building projects, and require developers to set aside 25 percent of their new units specifically for "low-income" people making 60 percent of the AMI. In addition to breaking existing law and common practice, and possibly violating the Constitution's "takings" clause, Stringer's plan would make it completely uneconomical to build anything going forward.

Maya Wiley was Mayor de Blasio's counsel for three years. It was she who devised the "agents of the city" dodge to protect powerful political/corporate consultants from having their communications with the mayor disclosed. She also organized a deal with Google to allow the tech giant to install enormous surveillance monoliths called "kiosks" all around the city. These purportedly would provide free Wi-Fi to disadvantaged people, closing the "digital divide," though their only practical use was to let vagrants watch porn or YouTube videos until that feature was disabled. Wiley is a strong supporter of Black Lives Matter and protested the NYPD's efforts to arrest activist Derrick Ingram for, in her words, being "at a Black Lives Matter rally with a bullhorn, expressing himself." In fact, Ingram assaulted a cop by placing his megaphone against her ear and shouting into it, causing the officer severe pain and hearing loss. Wiley demanded that the NYPD commissioner resign for sending the police to arrest Ingram.

One might imagine that Brooklyn Borough President Eric Adams, a former NYPD detective, would prioritize public safety as a leading mayoral candidate. But he, too, has encouraged massive cuts to the police budget. During summer 2020, when New York City was flooded with illegal fireworks, Adams encouraged residents kept up all hours by incendiary explosions not to call the police. "This is a non-violent act, so those three numbers that we always dial— 911—get over that," Adams counseled, explaining that the point of the George Floyd protests was to end "over-aggressive police action."

Instead, Adams advised, people bothered by late-night fireworks displays ought to extend a neighborly hand to the unauthorized pyrotechnicians. "Go talk to the young people or the people on your block who are using fireworks," he suggested. "Maybe we should say 'good morning' to them. Maybe we should say, 'Hello, how was school? Do you need a summer job?'" One Brooklyn resident, Shatavia Walls, took Adams's advice. She asked a man to stop lighting fireworks outside the Pink Houses projects in East New York. Offended by her request, he shot her eight times, killing her.

Contrary to the commonly held idea that police invariably escalate tension and conflict, cops in fact spend most of their time defusing quarrels in which they have no personal stake. Their ability to maintain public order in an impersonal manner is exactly why people call them. Adams, a former cop, ought to understand this better than most.

It goes on, all the way down through the city council, to the stacks of people vying to join them. There's a common assumption that Bill de Blasio was a failure as mayor. But that's a question of perspective. What was he elected to do and by whom? If you are a city employee, he expanded your workforce, rewarded you with good contracts, and protected your job. If you run a political consultancy, he enriched you. If you work for an activist nonprofit organization, he supported you. If you are a hard-left activist or aspiring politician, he gave you a pivot to swing the city further left, because he didn't. He's only a failure by the standards of the 90 percent of the city who want to have a livable city with economic opportunity, good schools, and safe streets. And if you're in that group, well, you're out of luck, because it's not clear that you matter.

A return to livability and civility will take more than electing a "good person" as mayor. Are they making better people? Michael Bloomberg—a relatively nonideological technocrat, now seen as a kind of dream mayor by people who don't recognize that he pursued a growth agenda without enacting fundamental reform of the city's spending addiction—was a one-off: there are very few billionaires around willing to spend $100 million to squeak into office and then untold tens of millions more buying acquiescence from every civil society organization in the city.

People will need to organize voting blocs to demand livability, if that's what they want. The rights of the disorderly to make the streets unpleasant and unsafe cannot be allowed to veto the rights of the peaceable to enjoy calm and pleasant public spaces. The city will have to recognize that the rich are not the enemy of the poor but in fact are the ones who fund New York City's generous social services infrastructure. Big and small businesses alike must be given room to grow, and New York's leadership must resist the impulse to constrain enterprise with burdensome regulations. Otherwise, New York City will sink into disorder, dispossession, and bankruptcy. Bye-bye.

Coda: Anarchy in NYC

.

A FTER TRUMP'S ATTORNEY GENERAL William Barr des-
ignated New York, along with Portland and Seattle, as
"anarchistic" cities, de Blasio expressed outrage. He characterized it as a political attack on "black and brown cities"—
though Portland and Seattle are two of the whitest cities in
the nation—and denied that New York is remotely lawless
or otherwise anarchic.

It's true that New York City wouldn't be confused for
Tegucigalpa or Mogadishu. And its violent crime rate, while
soaring, is still much lower than that of Baltimore or St.
Louis, for instance. But comparing New York today with the
New York of even a few years ago makes clear that the city

is undergoing a serious fracturing of civic order—one trending toward further disintegration.

Late one night in July 2020, I was walking my dogs around Washington Square Park. Earlier that day, I had noticed a car with Florida plates and a curious open storage area on its roof, jerry-rigged together with brackets and chicken wire, holding an array of clothes, camping gear, and household goods. As I neared the car that night, I noted that its front door was open and that someone was sitting sideways in the driver's seat, holding something between his knees. As I passed, he raised a large, compound crossbow, took aim at me through its scope, and pivoted in his seat, tracking my movement.

As soon as I was out of his range of fire, I called the police, who arrested him. They seized his crossbow—loaded with a quarrel, or bolt—and also a machete. He was charged with menacing with a deadly weapon, a class A misdemeanor that could result in up to a year in jail. He was released on his own recognizance immediately, the only condition being that he had to obey a temporary restraining order keeping him from contacting me.

I looked him up on the Internet. He has a significant criminal history, including sexual violence and assault charges. He is also—in layman's terms—out of his mind. His Facebook profile includes a video of him demonstrating how long he can hold his arm over fire, titled, "I demand my retribution," as well as rants about Jesus, the devil, and the true meaning of AIDS.

It took about 10 minutes poking around on the web to find out that this guy is seriously disturbed and has a documented history of criminal violence. Yet a few hours after he had pointed a loaded deadly weapon at a stranger, the justice system in New York City turned him loose, back to live in his illegally modified car.

All this may not amount to "anarchy" in a purist's sense of the word, but it isn't the New York City that Bill de Blasio inherited either.

Acknowledgments

I RECEIVED A GREAT DEAL of help in writing this book. Thanks to Brian Anderson and Paul Beston for their constant support. Frank Weimann had the idea for the project and made it happen. Stephen Eide, Nicole Gelinas, Rafael Mangual, and Ray Domanico provided me with insight in their areas of expertise. Gary Tilzer helped me understand the system of money and influence that drives local politics. Emmett Hare's political awareness and instincts are unparalleled, and he has been of tremendous assistance to me for many years.

Tom Chase, Adam Weis, Kevin Schmidt, Jason Blum, and Pat Dixon encouraged me.

Marina and Juliet were especially helpful in our research trip to the Hall of Fame for Great Americans in the Bronx. Their subtle insight into the culture of New York City informed my every step.

Note: Some sections of this book were adapted from previously published work by the author that appeared in *City Journal*, the *New York Post*, the *New York Daily News*, and the *Wall Street Journal*.

Index

About the Author

SETH BARRON IS A New York City–based writer and editor who has written extensively about local politics and culture for many years. A decade in the financial industry gave him a front-row seat at the mortgage meltdown of 2008. His work as a political operative and blogger led him to work for a leading Progressive politician on the New York City Council, where he witnessed the corroded gears of municipal governance up close.

Cited by the *New York Times* as "an acute observer of the intricacies of city politics" and by Fox News's Tucker Carlson as "the world's expert on Bill de Blasio's un-impressiveness," Seth Barron is known for his acid pen and incisive outlook. His work has been published in *City Journal*, the *New York*

Post, the *New York Daily News,* and the *Wall Street Journal* and has been circulated widely. He appears on both national and local media frequently.

Having raised two children in the city through the public schools, Barron writes with an understanding of the needs and aspirations of ordinary New Yorkers. He serves as managing editor of *The American Mind,* a publication of the Claremont Institute.

Seth Barron lives with his wife in Manhattan.

This 384-page guide will show you how to:

- Get up to $103,200 MORE in Social Security payments
- Retire overseas on $1,250 a month or less
- Create your perfect retirement plan
- Boost your income in retirement
- Save THOUSANDS on Medicare and drug costs
- Know the best age for you to start collecting Social Security
- And much, much more!

To get your FREE copy of the *Baby Boomer Survival Guide* go to:

Boom511.com/NY

Simple **Heart Test**

FACT:

▸ Nearly half of those who die from heart attacks each year never showed prior symptoms of heart disease.

▸ If you suffer cardiac arrest outside of a hospital, you have just a 7% chance of survival.

Don't be caught off guard. Know your risk now.

TAKE THE TEST NOW ...

Renowned cardiologist **Dr. Chauncey Crandall** has partnered with **Newsmaxhealth.com** to create a simple, easy-to-complete, online test that will help you understand your heart attack risk factors. Dr. Crandall is the author of the #1 best-seller *The Simple Heart Cure: The 90-Day Program to Stop and Reverse Heart Disease.*

Take Dr. Crandall's Simple Heart Test — it takes just 2 minutes or less to complete — it could save your life!

Discover your risk now.

- **Where you score on our unique heart disease risk scale**
- Which of your lifestyle habits really protect your heart
- **The true role your height and weight play in heart attack risk**
- Little-known conditions that impact heart health
- **Plus much more!**

SimpleHeartTest.com/NY